W9-AMT-158

Undisruptable

Undisruptable

A Mindset of Permanent Reinvention for Individuals, Organisations and Life

Aidan McCullen

WILEY

Library of Congress Cataloging-in-Publication Data is Available

ISBN 9781119770480 (hardback) ISBN 9781119817093 (ePub)
ISBN 9781119817109 (ePDF)

Cover Design: Wiley

Set in 12/15pt and JansonTextLTStd by SPi Global, Chennai, India

SKYC1719E1C-A388-4D6E-9329-6711C913979A_060821

To my wonderful wife, Niamh and sons, Josh and Jake.
Thank you for all your love and support and
for putting up with my crazy stories.

Contents

Foreword by Dee Hock, founder and CEO Emeritus of VISA

Out of the lumber of things we are taught, the gravel of our experience and the cement of the things we observe, we slowly erect an edifice, an unconscious, internal model of reality. We gradually fill it with the furniture of habit, custom, belief, and bias. We get comfortable there. It's our sanctuary. Through its windows, small and distorted as they may be, we view society and the world. Our internal model of reality is how we make sense of the world, and it can be a badly built place indeed. Even if it is well constructed, it may have become archaic. Everything that gave rise to it may have changed, since the natural world and human society are never stagnant. They are constantly becoming.

During the past four decades the external world has been changing at a rate enormously greater than the rate at which our internal models have been evolving. Nothing behaves as we think it should. Nothing makes sense. At such times the world appears to be staging a madhouse. It is never a madhouse. It is merely the great tide of evolution in temporary flood, moving this way and that, piling up against that which obstructs its flow, trying to break loose and sweep away the internal model that opposes it.

At such times, we experience extreme dissonance and stress. At the heart of that dissonance and stress is paradox. The more powerful and entrenched our internal model of reality, the more difficult it is to perceive and understand the fundamental nature of the changed world we experience. Yet without such perception and understanding it is extremely difficult to understand

and change our internal model. This is precisely where we are today, and it is rapidly getting worse.

Deep in most of us, below our awareness, indelibly implanted there by three centuries of the Industrial Age, is the mechanistic, separatist, cause-and-effect, command-and-control, machine model of reality. People are more than machines. The universe is more than a clock. Nature is more than a sequence of cogs and wheels. Nor is it a collection of bits and bytes. Numbers are not values. Mathematics can never be the measure of all things. Words and syllables are not reality. And science is not a deity. All human knowledge is an approximation, useful at times, foolish at others.

When our internal model of reality is in conflict with rapidly changing external realities, there are three ways to respond: First, we can cling to our old internal model and attempt to impose it on external conditions in a futile attempt to make them conform to our expectations. That is what our present mechanistic, societal institutions compel us to attempt, and what we continually dissipate our ingenuity and ability trying to achieve. Attempting to impose an archaic internal model on a changed external world is futile.

Second, we can engage in denial. We can refuse to accept the new external reality. We can pretend that external changes are not as profound as they really are. We can deny that we have an internal model, or that it bears examination. When the world about us appears to be irrational, erratic, and irresponsible, it is all too easy to blame others for the unpleasant, destructive things we experience. It is equally easy to abandon meaning, engage in erratic behaviour, or retreat into fantasy. All such is also futile.

Third, we can attempt to understand and change our internal model of reality. That is the least common alternative, and for good reason. Changing an internal model of reality is extremely difficult, terrifying, and complex. It requires a meticulous, painful examination of beliefs. It requires a fundamental understanding of consciousness and how it must change. It destroys our sense of time and place. It calls into question our very identity. We can never be sure of our place, or our value, in a new order of things. We may lose sight of who and what we are.

Changing our internal model of reality requires an enormous act of faith, for it requires time to develop, and we require time to grow into it. Yet it is the only workable answer. We are not helpless victims in the grasp of some supernatural force. We were active participants in the creation of our present consciousness.

From that consciousness we created our present internal model of reality which is increasingly archaic. To change our internal model of reality will take time.

It will require great respect for the past, vast understanding and tolerance of the present, and even greater belief and trust in the future. It is an odyssey that calls out to the best among us, and the best within us, one and all.

No one should be condemned for failure to welcome change. It is a pervasive problem which plagues us all. Dostoevsky put it into perspective in the last century when he wrote: 'Taking a new step, uttering a new word is what people fear most'.

The undeniable fact is that we have created the greatest explosion of capacity to receive, store, utilise, transform, and transmit information in history and that is causing an even greater explosion in societal diversity and complexity. There is no way to turn back. Whether we recognise it or not, whether we will it or not, whether we welcome it or not, we are caught up in the most profound change in the history of civilisation. If you think to perpetuate the old ways, try to recall the last time evolution rang your number to ask your consent.

Life is uncertainty, surprise, hate, wonder, speculation, love, joy, pain, mystery, beauty, and a thousand other things – some we can't even imagine. Control requires denial of life. Life is not about certainty or controlling. It's not about getting. It's not about having. It's not about knowing. It's not even about being. Life is eternal perpetual becoming or it is nothing. Becoming is not a thing to be known, commanded, or controlled. It is a magnificent, mysterious, odyssey to be experienced.

Aidan McCullen has lived a fascinating life of major change. In his book, *Undisruptable*, he brings us a method for making sense of the external world, and an accessible and visual approach to letting go of the past, and welcoming the future with a mind-set of permanent reinvention. It is a timely, thoughtful book, well worth reading.

Dee Hock, founder and CEO Emeritus of VISA and author of *One from Many: VISA and the Rise of Chaordic Organization*, November 2020.

Introduction: Why You Should Read This Book

It seemed as if time stood still as the ball spun towards me. I thought to myself, *You did it man. You achieved your goal; you are in the starting line-up for one of the best teams in the world.* I caught the ball, brushed off some would-be tacklers and made some ground. After the game, the coach, the club president and my new teammates congratulated me on a great performance. I was off to the dream start. Little did I know how that peak moment was the start of a steep decline. One year later, after multiple injuries, disappointments and setbacks, I joined a lesser club. Two years after that, I reached the end of the career I had built over a decade.

That same year, Forbes magazine ran a cover story entitled 'One billion customers, can anyone catch the cell phone king?' It was November 2007. Nokia's stock surged one hundred and fifty-five percent with a peak price of over forty dollars per share. Nokia was the largest mobile phone company in the world, dominating more than fifty percent of the global market. Two years later, the share price dropped below ten dollars per share. Eight years after that, shares plummeted below five dollars and Nokia offloaded its smartphone business to Microsoft. In the period of only six years, Nokia saw their market share slip from fifty percent in 2007 to three percent in 2013. A powerful business, built slowly over decades, faced a dramatic descent that lasted less than a decade.

My sports career and Nokia's fate share similar patterns common to disruption. The moment we reach the peak in any endeavour, the dip is already underway. The difficulty lies in recognising when we have reached the peak and what we can do to prevent the decline.

Looking back on my sports career, I can identify numerous things I might have done differently – one of the many benefits of hindsight. There is no doubt that Nokia's leadership identified many decisions they should have taken, or not as the case may be. Perhaps they should have paid more attention to the threat of the iPhone? They might have reinvented their business while they were on top? After all, they had developed a prototype smart phone and even conceptualised an app store, but decided to focus on updating the existing models that had made them successful in the first place. These are common 'might have' considerations we see with all disruption. Kodak might have prepared for a digital world like Fujifilm did. Microsoft might have entered the hardware business earlier. Blackberry might have diversified their portfolio.

Alas, therein lies the problem: our successes often blind us to the possibility of failure, our victories can sometimes defeat us. When organisations are at their most profitable, they are also at their most fragile. When individuals are at their most successful, we are also at our most vulnerable. We become so preoccupied with optimising, enjoying and defending the competitive advantage that made us successful today that we neglect to prepare for tomorrow. This mode of thinking is outdated. Too much has changed in the last two decades and will change at a faster pace in the coming years. We can no longer win with defence alone, there is no longer a safe harbour for organisations, there is no longer a career destination for individuals. Businesses and careers, like life, are about perpetual *becoming*, a permanent reinvention.

Happily for me, there was one major difference between Nokia's organisational fate and my professional rugby fate: I knew when the end was coming. Although those final years of my career were difficult, they afforded me ample time to prepare for the ambiguous future that awaits every sports person after retirement. I had time to explore burgeoning industries that I could enter. I had time to develop capabilities before I would need them and research which career paths would provide the greatest growth opportunities. I had no choice but to reinvent. After all, my career was over and I had nothing to lose. Nokia, on the other hand, had everything to lose.

That is so often the challenge: we resist reinvention for fear of losing the competitive advantage we have developed. The harder fought our successes, the stronger we defend them. Rather than diversify when they had sufficient revenue and resources to do so, Nokia held on tightly to what they had already created and ignored intensifying threats.

Once-dominant companies will experience the fate of Nokia with increasing frequency unless permanent reinvention becomes part of business as usual. The key, we will see, is to reinvent in permanence. We can no longer wait until we reach a stall point in our lifecycle to explore new possibilities – that is too late. We must build a constant flow of reinvention initiatives into business, careers and life.

Seventy-five percent of transformation programmes fail, highlighting that even when leaders recognise the need to reinvent, the status quo prevails. This failure rate is not exclusive to organisations. As the majority of us have experienced, as much as eighty percent of New Year's resolutions also fail. Even when we know new habits will benefit us greatly, we fail to adapt. Why is this, and how can we improve the odds?

My personal experience with reinvention, the lessons from a sporting career, coupled with various transformation roles, inspired me to seek answers. With a particular fascination with mindset, I researched widely the fields of neuroscience, organisational transformation, innovation, philosophy, epigenetics and human evolution to understand how we can succeed. This book is the culmination of a decade of this research and hundreds of interviews with some of the best minds on the planet.

My findings continuously point to a common trend: *we cannot change what we do until we also change how we think*. Within organisations this translates as: *we cannot change business models until we also change mental models*. Throughout the book, you will see this strong interconnection between individual change and organisational change, because they are symbiotic.

The underlying questions I pose are:

'How do we navigate a world that is changing at breakneck speed, as business leaders, and as individuals?'

'What can we do to minimise the impact of disruption on our careers, in our organisations and on our lives?'

The answer I propose lies with a mindset: a mindset of permanent reinvention.

What is the Permanent Reinvention Mindset?

Think back to when you had an eye test. Do you remember how the optometrist placed a contraption over your eyes and added a series of lenses to test your vision? That contraption is like a world view – the way we perceive the world, other people, and our overall philosophies of life. Every time we add a lens, it modifies how we experience the world. The difference between that contraption and a world view is that each time a new lens is

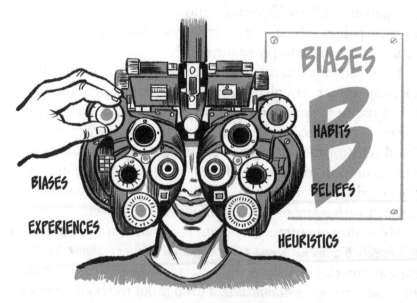

Figure 0.1   The Optometrist's contraption

added to our world view, the lenses remain in place. We must be vigilant about the lenses we admit, because they colour our view of the world, sometimes to our benefit and sometimes not. They can limit us, encourage us to seek confirming evidence, and make us hold on to mental models, business models and convictions even when they no longer serve us.

In this analogy, the brain plays the role of the optometrist adding lenses as we learn and experience new things. Over time, the lenses amass to create a worldview unique to each one of us, and heavily influenced by those around us.

As we grow older, our lenses pile up through education and media, religion and politics, friends and foes, poverty and prosperity, society and culture and countless other ways. Psychologists tell us that by the time we reach age thirty-five, our behaviours, attitudes, beliefs, emotional reactions, habits, skills, associative memories, conditioned responses, and perceptions are subconsciously programmed within us. Although we collect and use many of these lenses subconsciously, we can be deliberate about updating them.

As we advance through life, our lenses become scratched and worn and distort our view, blinding us to both threats and opportunities. 'Any real change', novelist James Baldwin wrote, 'implies the breakup of the world as one has always known it, the loss of all that gave one an identity, the end of safety'. Baldwin chose his words carefully. The 'real change' he mentions is transformational change, like a caterpillar becoming a butterfly. It is a change of state. This is the kind of change we must deliberately pursue. However, such change invokes resistance and involves letting go of the old self to make way for the new. Meaningful transformations involve a multitude of emotions, many obstacles and immense resistance from the status quo.

The purpose of this book is to offer a series of new lenses, to update our conceptual story of change as organisations and individuals. When we shift how we perceive the process of transformation, we can embrace it more fully. By recognising the common pitfalls, resistance and blockers to change, we become more at ease with the ambiguity that is synonymous with today's world.

As you read this book, consider each chapter as a new lens. Over the course of the book, the lenses compound to culminate with the permanent reinvention mindset.

Why Reinvent?

'I can't think of any period in human history when people were really certain what to do, had no surprises and no unexpected developments. What is novel is not uncertainty; what is novel is a realization that uncertainty is here to stay. . .[Therefore], we are challenged with a task, which I think is unprecedented — and the task is to develop an art, to develop an art of living permanently with uncertainty.'

— Zygmunt Bauman

According to the Boston Consulting Group, the average life of a business model was once fifteen years. By their estimation, that number has drastically reduced to five years. A study released by Innosight, the Corporate Longevity Forecast, predicts the average tenure of companies on the S&P 500 list will continue to grow shorter and shorter over the next decade. Innosight reported that the thirty-three-year average tenure of companies on the S&P 500 in 1964 had narrowed to twenty-four by 2016. They forecast it will shrink to only twelve years by 2027. Further research, conducted by Credit Suisse, revealed that the average time a company spends in the Fortune 500 has diminished from sixty years to less than twenty. These studies show that, even when you become one of the most successful companies in the world, it may not last. The Covid-19 pandemic, and a plethora of societal shifts including artificial intelligence, digitisation and globalization, will greatly accelerate these downward spirals.

This reality does not escape the leaders of the world's most powerful organisations. Amazon founder, Jeff Bezos told employees at an all-hands meeting in May 2020 that Amazon is not 'too big to fail'. Bezos was responding was to a question about the lessons he had learned from the bankruptcies of Sears and other victims of the retail apocalypse. His response is a warning for all of us to understand that disruption is part of the new reality. He said, 'Amazon is not too big to fail. In fact, I predict one day Amazon will fail. Amazon will go bankrupt. If you look at large companies, their lifespans tend to be thirty-plus years, not a hundred-plus years'. When the CEO of one of the most successful organisations of all time and one of the richest men in the world says his company will not last, we should pay attention.

One of the challenges for so many organisations and individuals is that we have been educated and prepared for a steady and stable environment. The relative stability of the post-war period, an anomalous period in world history, has somewhat contributed to our conditioning for stability. Our mental and operational flexibility has atrophied.

Many of the victims of shrinking corporate lifespans failed to change with the times. Today's business environment is far from predictable and can be characterised by the acronym VUCA. VUCA was introduced by the U.S. Army War College to describe a more volatile, uncertain, complex and ambiguous world resulting from the Cold War. Throughout the book, I will refer to the times we are in as 'VUCA times'. The term has grown in popularity in recent years as we experience multiple disruptions driven by socio-economic change, political turmoil and increasing business and individual disruption. Vladimir Lenin once said, 'There are decades where nothing happens, and there are weeks where decades happen'. Today, it feels like decades are happening weekly. This rate of change can feel overwhelming and difficult to comprehend, but there are patterns in the chaos.

With regards to this speed of change, many commentators frequently use the term exponential change. Many of us understand exponential to mean 'extremely fast'. That is not the case. Exponential growth is deceptive, back-loaded and catches us off guard. In this VUCA age, it is important to grasp its meaning, because it is a contributing force behind so much of the change we are experiencing.

The Exponential Rate of Change

Exponential growth explains growth rate where quantities increase slowly at first, growing at an accelerated rate. We witnessed exponential growth rate with the spread of Covid-19 across the planet. Later growth takes us by surprise and catches individuals and organisations off guard. Often the starting point is so small and moves at a slow pace that we take our eye off that growth as we deem it unimportant. Exponential growth is back-loaded, which helps explain another phenomenon, known as Amara's Law, after the scientist Roy Amara. This law states we overestimate the effect of a technology in the short term and underestimate the effect in the long term. The phenomenon of exponential growth was initially described by Intel co-founder Gordon Moore. When observing the evolution of computer processors, Moore observed three distinct variables:

1. They doubled their computing power.
2. They became half as expensive.
3. They halved in size.

Moore noticed that this happened every eighteen to twenty-four months. We can understand the impact of exponential change by looking to the Apollo space missions in the 1970s. The guidance computer that powered those missions was less powerful than an early smartphone. That seems ridiculous, perhaps even impossible, but it is precisely the point about exponential growth of technology: it is deceptive.

Imagine you are working in Nasa in 1969. The guidance computer is a marvellous technological feat, it is ground-breaking technology. You cannot perceive anything better – you are limited by your field of vision. When we achieve the best possible standards for a specific point in time, our success blinds us to future change.

Today, the smartphone in your pocket is more powerful than all the computer power in NASA fifty years ago. That smartphone

Figure 0.2   Exponential change

power is increasing exponentially. Many technologies that were figments of the imagination of science fiction writers will become a reality within the coming decades. Such change removes the comfort of predictability. To ensure you fully grasp the concept of exponential growth, the following thought experiment is useful.

Imagine you are seated in the highest seat in the top row of a sports stadium. The stadium is watertight. On the pitch below you see a match official holding a small water dropper. She releases a single drop of water on the pitch. After one minute, she releases two more drops. A minute later four drops, and she continues to double the drops every minute. The quantity of water continues in a pattern of doublings every minute. This sequence of doublings is the exponential rate of change. If the official continues to double the number of drops every minute (exponentially), how long will it take to fill the entire stadium? Weeks? Days? Hours? Minutes?

From the very first drop, to completely filling the stadium would take a mere forty-nine minutes! But here is the rub, and why exponential change is so deceptive. How long do you think it would take for the water to reach those people sitting pitchside, on the lowest level of seats in the stadium? This part takes forty-five of the forty-nine minutes. This leaves you with a mere four minutes to escape. Think about that for a moment, what does it mean?

When you and those seated on the upper rows of the stadium realise there is a problem, you think you have enough time to take action. After all, you see that the water took forty-five minutes to reach the people at ground level. At that stage, the stadium is only seven percent full, surely you have sufficient time to escape? However, as the water continues to fill the stadium at an exponential rate, it causes panic, fear and chaos. In this state of fear and panic, our decision making is flawed and we make poor decisions.

This is what happens when industries adopt a defensive approach to business, believing change will not catch them off guard. This is what happens when organisations ignore evolving customer needs and business models. This is what happens when individuals stop learning and do not develop new capabilities before they need them.

When organisations and industries experience what appears to be sudden disruption, they respond with disbelief. In 2016, Nokia CEO Stephen Elop announced Microsoft's acquisition of Nokia's mobile phone division. Elop ended his speech saying, 'We did nothing wrong, but somehow, we lost'. A decade earlier, Nokia was the cell phone king. This is a common trend where a once successful organisation falls from the peak of success. The once-celebrated poster child of success becomes a case study of disruption and the list of such companies will get increasingly longer and at a faster pace.

Former CEO of General Electric Jack Welch said, 'If the rate of change on the outside exceeds the rate of change on the inside, the end is near'. Welch warned when businesses do not keep pace with the speed of change in their marketplace, they face extinction, as Nokia discovered. We must remember that an organisation is a mass of people and an organisation cannot change if the people within that organisation resist change.

While there is an increasing onus on organisations to provide growth opportunities for their people to adapt to these changes, it is our responsibility to take charge of our own personal and professional growth.

Personal Transformation

Throughout this book, I propose that we must prepare for inevitable and perpetual change. The key is to change long before we need to, because when we need it, it is often too late. We must embrace change as a constant and adopt a mindset of permanent reinvention. To understand this mindset, we will explore case studies of failures and successes. We will see how we must be vigilant to the signals of change and by doing so can ensure we become undisruptable as organisations and individuals.

As the lifespan of organisations plummets, so too do the capabilities of the people who work in those organisations. In 1942, Austrian economist Joseph Schumpeter introduced the concept of *Creative Destruction*. According to Schumpeter, the creation of any new value brings the destruction of the old. Think how the Covid-19 pandemic saw the decline of some industries and the stellar growth of others. Today, we are experiencing creative destruction at an alarming rate. As industries collapse and others emerge, many professionals will continue to find their skills outdated or unnecessary. One day they are enjoying their peak, the next they find themselves replaced by more cost-efficient solutions such as artificial intelligence.

The 2018 IBM skills gap study reports that over 120 million workers in the world's twelve largest economies will need to upskill in the next three years due to the impact of artificial intelligence. In 2016, the same study revealed the top desired skill was digital knowledge and STEM skills (Science, Technology, Engineering, Maths). Only two years later, the top desired skill was 'A willingness to be flexible, agile and adaptable to change'. This willingness to be flexible, agile and adaptable to change is at the heart of permanent reinvention. Unfortunately, not everyone is willing to adapt. Some will resist, some will not see change coming, while others will stick their head in the sand and hope that the storm will pass. The most common reason that change initiatives fail is *not* that people don't recognise the need to change. It is that they are incapable of doing so. A mindset of permanent reinvention will give you a new set of lenses and a new way of embracing change. The first step is to recognise why we resist change and a new mindset will then help us to embrace it.

Reading the Tides

In 1855, Matthew Fontaine Maury published the first book on Oceanography. When a leg injury left Maury unfit for sea duty, he devoted his time to the study of navigation, meteorology, winds, and currents and became known as 'The Pathfinder of the Seas'. Maury observed patterns in logbooks left by sea captains travelling the North Atlantic. The captains recorded their daily locations, and the speed of winds and currents. Maury extended his research by asking sailors to put messages in bottles. The message noted the ship's location when the bottle was thrown overboard. When the bottles washed ashore, the captains asked the finders to send Maury a note telling him where they found the bottle. In this way, Maury could figure out more detailed ocean current patterns and add them to his charts.

As Maury discovered eventually everything displays a pattern, but you have to know what to look for. When you can identify patterns, you can harness them to your advantage.

If you think this is a skill reserved for the domain of experts like Maury, it is not the case. To illustrate how even a basic understanding of patterns can stack the odds in your favour, consider the beautiful example of ten-year-old Tilly Smith from Surrey, England.

In 2004, the Smith family was on Maikhao beach in Phuket, Thailand. Having recently learned about tsunamis in school, Tilly recognised the patterns: receding water from the shoreline and frothing bubbles on the surface were strong signals. When she alerted her parents, they quickly warned others on the beach and the staff at their hotel. Everyone left the beach just before the tsunami devastated the shoreline. Thanks to Tilly's basic understanding of the patterns of tsunamis, there were no casualties. Tsunamis are difficult to predict, even for experts, but they exhibit patterns that are recognisable if you know what to look for. Tsunamis are like exponential change; they appear suddenly and by the time people realise there is a problem it is often too late.

A tsunami of digitisation, Moore's law, artificial intelligence, data, globalisation, climate change and pandemics is already upon us. Over the coming decade, we will experience more change than we have in the last century. It will happen at an increasingly faster pace. Covid-19 will accelerate digitisation, automation and the adoption of artificial intelligence. We cannot predict what will happen nor when, but we can prepare for the change.

We can attempt to erect a protective moat around our careers, our expertise or our business plan, but the waves of change will batter it down.

We can stick our head in the sands and hope the tsunamis of change will spare us, but the odds are not good.

The alternative is really our only chance of survival. We must learn to understand the trends and surf the waves of change.

> As the Chinese proverb tells us, 'When the wind of change blows, some build walls, while others build windmills'.
>
> —Chinese Proverb.

This book shares the mindset of how to build windmills.

Overview of Undisruptable

Rather than a rigid set of frameworks or business models, I present the book as a series of mental models. To bring these mental models to life, I offer analogies from nature, anecdotes from business, ancient wisdom, exemplars of perpetual change and evidence from evolution, neuroscience, business and life.

For the experienced changemaker, this book will provide an enjoyable way to associate the various concepts you already understand with fresh analogies offered throughout. For the reader who wants to learn more about disruption, why it happens and how you can navigate the turbulent waters ahead, the book offers a set of lenses that will help you make sense of this change. The ultimate aim is to adopt a mindset of permanent reinvention. The chapters are deliberately short and visual, adapted for our changing lifestyles. I hope that you can read each chapter over a coffee break and come away with a valuable lens or a renewed way to better understand a lens you already possess.

Part One begins with why we resist change. Leading change is not a trivial task; you'll face resistance, whether it be personal transformation or organisational change. It is important to understand the challenges before we encounter them. Next, we introduce the S curve as a mental model or heuristic to understand a large variety of phenomena. I extend this concept to update the S curve model and introduce the 'infinity curve'. The infinity curve suggests that we must reinvent in permanence, not just at a certain point on the S curve, because we never quite understand when we have reached our peak until it has already happened. When corporate life spans were longer, businesses could afford to reinvent at specific times in their life cycles. The speed of change and disruption that we are experiencing today no longer affords us this luxury. We can think of the infinity curve as the optometrist's contraption on which to hang the new lenses we will adopt throughout the book.

Part 2 highlights characteristics of the permanent reinvention mindset. These are traits common to undisruptable companies and individuals. The lenses here include analogies, research, examples and high-level case studies. We see how *undisruptables*, those exemplars of permanent reinvention, approach mistakes, how they build capability before they need it, how they willingly reinvent, how they expect and deal with setbacks and how they embrace fear. We pay particular attention to the vital role of vision.

Part 3 brings the mindset to life. We see how Fujifilm reinvented long before they needed to and how they unbundled and rebundled capabilities to achieve phenomenal results. We will see how Nokia and Blackberry failed to reinvent, even after they achieved the heights of success. We celebrate undisruptable individuals like Arnold Schwarzenegger, Josephine Cochrane and Walt Disney and use the S curve to map their mindset of permanent reinvention.

Finally, we end our journey with the most important lens of all. That is that every rebirth requires some form of death. While the past plays a noble role in the future, we must let go of the past to make room for that future.

Let the reinventing begin!

PART 1

Permanent
Reinvention Framework

1

Resistance to Reinvention

Figure 1.1 Using the former self to fuel the future self

'We delight in the beauty of the butterfly, but rarely admit the changes it has gone through to achieve that beauty.'
—Maya Angelou

After hatching, caterpillars eat their own eggshells as fuel to power their future transformation. Caterpillars outgrow their exoskeleton several times as they mature, before something deep within them signals that it is time for a bigger change. This signal starts with a deep impulse, an inkling at a cellular level, programmed deep in its DNA. The cells that initiate the change are aptly called *imaginal discs*, from the word imagination.

Imaginal discs begin life as single-celled organisms and remain dormant until they instinctively awaken when it is time for metamorphosis. Imaginal cells are so unlike the caterpillar's cells that the immune system attacks them as invaders. Despite being rejected by the organism, imaginal cells persevere, multiplying within the caterpillar. These new cells resonate at the same frequency, communicating and coordinating to overwhelm the caterpillar's immune system. They induce the caterpillar to find a twig and harden its skin, which acts as a cocoon. This is when a caterpillar becomes a chrysalis. Then, the caterpillar goes through a beautiful transformation by dissolving into a nutritious liquid that fuels the metamorphosis into a butterfly.

Just as the caterpillar used its eggshell as fuel, the butterfly now uses the caterpillar to power its future. For the new being to emerge, it does not destroy the old, but rather builds upon what was already there. The old plays a noble role in enabling the new.

Transformational Change or Incremental Change?

In personal and organisational transformation, we often forget that becoming something new involves letting go of something old. That may sound easy, but it can mean letting go of an outdated business model, it may mean a change in status and compensation for the people in your organisation. None of these changes are easy. By its very nature the status quo does not give up without a fight, much like the cells of the caterpillar resisting the imaginal cells. This battle, this tension is the hallmark of transformational change. Incremental change is a cakewalk in comparison, like the caterpillar growing larger as it eats.

Incremental change is characterised by minor improvements such as the latest version of the iPhone. Transformational change is the transition from a Nokia or BlackBerry to the iPhone or the horse to the car. Transformation involves psychological warfare between the existing and the emergent.

Corporate changemakers can be forgiven when they label their legacy organisations and colleagues as blockers of progress who are 'stuck in their ways'. While it is understandable that those who drive change become frustrated with those who resist it, we must recognise that it is the legacy organisation that fuels the emergent one. Apart from funding, we may eventually need any mix of logistics, marketing, institutional knowledge, personnel, and other supports from the old to fuel the new.

Just as imaginal cells are different from the caterpillar's cells, changemakers within large organisations have different mindsets. Corporate innovators think differently, have a greater risk tolerance and see opportunities and threats where others may not. If you are an innovator, interactions with those in positions of power from the legacy organisation are draining and feel like a battle. Well, that's because it *is* a battle and one that you will lose unless you can gain support from other imaginal cells within the corporate body. However, we must realise that they are also playing their role as corporate antibodies.

A changemaker represents a threat; foreign DNA is perceived as an attack on the existing entity and triggers an immune response. When a changemaker reaches this point, they should reframe it as a mark of progress. If you do not reach this point of resistance, it might be a sign that you are not pushing the boundaries far enough. See this resistance as a milestone and not a mill stone.

This is where we can learn from the imaginal cells of the caterpillar. If we create an army of imaginal cells, an army which resonates at a different frequency, we can attract those who resonate at the same frequency as us. Organisations who expect change to happen after a corporate retreat with some flip charts and Post-it notes are confusing real change with cosmetic change. Such initiatives are like a splash, while transformation creates a ripple that spreads and persists over time. Creating a ripple is a slower and much more frustrating process, especially for the change-maker, but it is the only way to create a lasting transformation. In time, habits will change and so too will mindsets. Eventually, enough cells will fuse to overpower the legacy organisation, and you will experience a metamorphosis.

When we encounter transformation at a personal level, we undergo a process similar to the caterpillar and the organisation. Deep down, we feel the need to change – an inkling deep within us. Alas, very few of us listen for the impulse. Instead, we drown it out with 'busyness', alcohol or Netflix binges. Often unknowingly, we battle change, just like the caterpillar's immune system battles the imaginal cells. This is a perfectly natural part of the change process. The bigger the change, the greater the resistance. Even in the face of a devastating crisis, we still resist change.

For organisations, crisis may come in the form of a declining industry, a disruptive competitor or a recession resulting from a pandemic. For individuals, it might be a redundancy, the death of a loved one or an unexpected health issue. Whatever the case, when such crises arrive, many of us cannot or will not adapt.

> *'If you look at people after coronary-artery bypass grafting two years later, 90% of them have not changed their lifestyle'.*
> —Edward Miller, former CEO of Johns Hopkins Medicine

Cardiovascular disease accounts for almost 50,000 of the 150,000 daily deaths worldwide[1]. Despite such a high death rate, considerable research[2] shows that ninety percent of cardiovascular-related patients will not make the lifestyle changes required

---

[1] https://ourworldindata.org/causes-of-deathhttps://www.weforum.org/agenda/2020/05/how-many-people-die-each-day-covid-19-coronavirus/
[2] 90% of people won't change, Edward Miller, former CEO of Johns Hopkins Medicine: Change or Die (Regan, 2007) https://www.amazon.co.uk/Change-Die-Three-Keys-Work/dp/0061373672/

Figure 1.2   brain rejects new ideas

to reduce the chances of another event. Even when faced with such life-or-death situations, only ten percent can adapt. When confronted with such figures, is it any wonder that seventy-five percent of organisational transformation efforts fail? Organisations are a mass of people and if we resist such vital change in our personal lives, is it any surprise that we resist change in our work lives?

Peter Medawar[3] is regarded as the 'father of transplantation'. His work on graft rejection and immune tolerance is fundamental to the medical practice of tissue and organ transplants. Amidst all his work on our physiological immune responses, it is Medawar's remark about the human mind that speaks volumes. He said, 'The human mind treats a new idea the same way the body treats a strange protein; it rejects it'. In the same way, personal and organisational change encounter constant resistance and rejection.

Throughout the chapters that follow, you will add the lenses of the permanent reinvention mindset. Each lens will enable you

---

[3] https://en.wikipedia.org/wiki/Peter_Medawar

to see the need for transformation more clearly and understand why we resist change. When we understand such phenomena, we resist them less and become more capable of transformation. So, let's add the first lens, 'kintsugi thinking'.

Chapter One Takeaways

- Resisting change is natural.
- The status quo will always resist; that is its nature.
- Changemakers must recognise the signs of resistance as milestones of change; this resistance is a rite of passage.
- Incremental change means small improvements or minor changes.
- Transformational change can be extremely difficult and even painful.
- Transformational change involves psychological warfare for the individual.
- Even when faced with debilitating disease, many people still resist change.
- Even when faced with organisational disruption, many leaders resist reinvention.
- Transformational change involves territorial warfare for the organisation.
- Transformational change is a slow process that cannot be rushed.
- Becoming something new means letting go of something old.
- To create a new reality, we must introduce new thoughts and new practices to reinforce those new thoughts. This is the beginning of new mental models changing new business models; it is a circular process.
- The old self is fuel for the new like the caterpillar feeds on its shell and just like the butterfly feeds on its former self when it liquifies the caterpillar.

Considerations

For the individual

- What is my appetite for change?
- Are the changes I have made incremental or transformational?
- Do I block others when they seek transformational change?
- Write down three occasions when you have made transformational change in your life.
- If you can do this, think about the milestones of resistance that you experienced.
- Did others discourage you?
- Did you discourage yourself?
- What was your self-talk?
- What helped you get through?
- Was it an inkling from within?
- If you cannot identify any transformational change, that is OK.
- Write down transformational change that you would like to pursue.
- Listen to your resistance.
- What is blocking you?

For the organisation

- Are you mistaking incremental improvements with transformational change?
- Where is the resistance coming from?
- When the resistance comes, is it due to status or compensation or both?
- Do you have a deep inkling that your organisation needs to change?

- Sit with that inkling and let it emerge; don't resist it.
- Find the imaginal cells within your organisation: bring them together, listen to them, empower them and protect them.
- Brainstorm with your imaginal cells; what needs to happen for transformation to begin?

2

Kintsugi Thinking

Figure 2.1 Kintsugi thinking

'There is a crack in everything. That's how the light gets in'.
— Leonard Cohen

The Japanese word Kintsugi literally means golden ('kin') repair ('tsugi'). Kintsugi is the Japanese art of repairing broken pottery and ceramics with lacquer dusted or mixed with powdered gold, silver or platinum. As a philosophy, it treats breakage and repair as an integral part of an object's history. What is damaged, scarred and vulnerable is something to celebrate, rather than disguise. With kintsugi repairs, you can see the broken line; the line is celebrated and emphasised rather than hidden.

I call the mindset of reframing flaws and setbacks *Kintsugi Thinking*. It is a valuable lens through which to see the world. In our increasingly VUCA (Volatile, Uncertain, Complex, Ambiguous) world, we will need to experiment as we explore the future and to do that successfully we must learn to embrace mistakes.

Mistakes are the foundation on which we learn. We are not always going to get it right. Things are not going to go as we planned. We need to approach every attempt as an experiment. We can keep experimenting our way closer and closer to figuring out which things are going to work and which are not. Mistakes can channel our thinking toward success, if we perceive them this way. Take for example, Toyota's culture. What sets the organisation apart is the way it encourages employees to be forthcoming about the mistakes they make or the problems they face. By encouraging open communication as a core value for decades, Toyota has made its culture remarkably tolerant of failure. Amazon also uses the philosophy of kintsugi thinking, although they do not call it that. Before we explore organisational kintsugi thinking, let's look at the individual. In particular, let's see how the metrics and incentives we use affect our results.

From Quantity Comes Quality

It was the beginning of the year, at a community college pottery class. The teacher divided the class into two groups.

She tasked the first group with creating as many pieces as possible over the course of the year. At the end of the year, she would grade group one on the quantity of pieces they produced.

Group two had a different assignment. She instructed group two to create a single perfect piece. She would grade them on technical excellence and sophistication.

When grading day arrived, the teacher judged the groups. To the surprise of the entire class, the group focused on quantity produced the best work.

The teacher shared her observations. She started with group one, the quantity group. Every time this group produced a pot, they identified mistakes quickly, corrected them and moved on. This group had fun, enjoyed working together and experimented with new techniques. There was no fear of failure, because they understood they would not be judged on their errors. Their working environment was psychologically safe, and everyone knew that mistakes were acceptable once they learned from those mistakes.

The teacher's observations for group two – the quality group – were entirely different. Their main focus was to minimise mistakes. They created very few pots, and the pots they did create were bland, dull, and generic. They worked in a fearful environment where tensions were high, and mistakes were not tolerated. The experiment proved to be a worthwhile exercise for everyone involved and provides a valuable lesson for us: that mistakes are a natural part of progress.

In the French movie *La Haine*, the protagonist Hubert Koundé says, '*L'important n'est pas la chute, c'est l'atterrissage'*. This translates to English as, 'The important thing is not the fall, it's the landing'. Progress and change only happen when we accept failure and we bounce back up after we fall.

How could we ever expect to be perfect the first time we do anything new? I tell my children this all the time. If you observe a child learn to walk or ride a bicycle, watch how it unfolds. When a child falls from a bicycle and skins their knees, they look to their parent's reaction. It is our reaction that teaches the child how to react. If we run and express fear that they might have hurt themselves, the child may cry and from then on understand that is how they should react. However, if we smile and encourage the child by celebrating their great attempt, they will get up and have another go and that will influence their mindset in the future.

None of us know exactly how the future will unfold professionally, in business and in life. Global pandemics, recessions, disruption, artificial intelligence and how they all interact is a complex web impossible to navigate flawlessly. Therefore, in a turbulent society, previously held knowledge is no longer enough; we need new mindsets. Kintsugi thinking is a crucial philosophy for individuals and for leaders, the higher the tolerance for mistakes, the more we will learn. As we will see next, leaders who genuinely support mistakes within their organisations can enjoy phenomenal results.

Amazon Extinguishes the Fire

Amazon is an organisation that exemplifies kintsugi thinking. Amazon founder Jeff Bezos is globally acclaimed as one of the most successful businesspeople on the planet. While success is reflected in Amazon's share price, a positive attitude toward failure is emblazoned in Bezos' letters to shareholders. In 2015, Amazon became the fastest company ever to reach $100 billion in sales. In his letter to shareholders[1], Bezos highlighted some key characteristics of Amazon's success.

> *'One area where I think we are especially distinctive is failure.*
>
> *I believe we are the best place in the world to fail (we have plenty of practice!), and failure and invention are inseparable twins.'*

---

[1] https://www.sec.gov/Archives/edgar/data/1018724/000119312516530910/d168744dex991.htm

He went on to say,

'To invent you have to experiment, and if you know in advance that it's going to work, it's not an experiment. Most large organisations embrace the idea of invention, but are not willing to suffer the string of failed experiments necessary to get there.'

If Bezos ever attended pottery classes, you can guess which group he belonged to:

'This long-tailed distribution of returns is why it's important to be bold. Big winners pay for so many experiments.'

There is a series of celebrated cracks in the Amazon story so far and a lot of investments didn't pay off: Amazon local, Amazon Destinations, Amazon Auctions, Askville, and Dash buttons. One particularly interesting mistake was the Fire Phone.

We know artificial intelligence (AI) will feature profoundly in our future – its role is evolving rapidly. As voice-controlled AI advances exponentially, we will be able to interact with a multitude of apps and services without the need for a screen. Some of us have already dabbled with elements of the smart home, from voice-controlled light switches to smart refrigerators and even smart dog food bowls (yes, they exist).

When you think of a smart home, your list will feature the Google-owned Nest, or products from Samsung and Apple, but Amazon's Alexa may be in your top three. What does that have to do with the Fire Phone flop? Quite a lot, in a kintsugi sense.

Amazon's Fire Phone was poorly received and Amazon finally (ahem) extinguished the Fire in 2015. It was an expensive failure for the company, resulting in a $170 million write-off. However, when you view the outcome through the lens of *kintsugi thinking*, the failure spawned positive consequences. There were assets in the ashes. If Amazon had succeeded with the Fire Phone, it would have followed in the footsteps of Apple, Samsung, Google and Microsoft. Amazon would have doubled down by adding voice-controlled AI as a layer within the phone. However, when the Fire failed to gain traction, they were left with capabilities that they deployed in new ways.

When Alexa no longer had a natural home in the Fire Phone, Amazon included Alexa in the Echo speaker. This focus as a smart speaker helped Amazon customers clearly understand the value proposition. Today, Alexa has become synonymous with the smart speaker to such an extent that we refer to the Echo smart speaker as an Alexa. Alexa has become a product in her own right and one that further deepens Amazon's connection to the consumer.

Amazon beautifully demonstrated a few key concepts here. The first is how Bezos proved himself as an undisruptable leader and exemplified the permanent reinvention mindset. The second is how the *kintsugi thinking* paid off. Let's start with Bezos.

How would you have reacted to product leader, Ian Freed when the Fire Phone failed? Jeff Bezos ensured Freed's attempt was celebrated. In fact, he said to Freed that he shouldn't lose a night's sleep over it. Bezos was proud that Freed took a risk and his innovations made their way into other products. In doing so, Bezos sent a powerful statement to Amazon employees. Equally, he sent an appealing message to outside talent: Amazon is a great place to experiment and to take risks. In talking about the experience, Ian Freed said he took a role in Amazon because he would have a chance to 'swing the bat, when the base was loaded'.

Bezos ensured this message was not lost on shareholders when he said, 'I believe we are the best place in the world to fail'. This act essentially powdered Freed in golden lacquer, just like a piece of kintsugi pottery.

When an organisation encounters a major setback, everyone sits up to see how leadership will react. When the business landscape was steady and predictable, and organisations simply executed known processes, mistakes were rarely tolerated. It is important to emphasise that mistakes are not acceptable (within reason) when it comes to executing on known outcomes or rote tasks. But business today is a mix of both executing what we know and experimenting with what we do not know. This duality of business will inevitably result in mistakes. The key is to review why the mistakes happened and what we can do with the learnings. (Equally important is to understand what made success, so it can be repeated.) In this new reality, the only controllable is us, how we respond to change. We must adapt our mindset and grow accustomed to making mistakes.

The second lesson to learn from the Fire is how the attempt yielded a positive outcome. When the Fire Phone did not work out, Amazon was left with voice recognition capabilities. The product leader, Ian Freed, was working on the Echo project concurrently to the Fire Phone, which meant that he could cross-pollinate ideas. When his team embarked on the journey of developing those capabilities, they were open to deploy them in ways that were not yet fully formed. In what Freed calls, 'swinging the bat', Amazon 'developed capabilities before they needed them'. Remember that phrase; it is core to the permanent reinvention mindset, and you will see it come to life throughout the book.

The Fire was an important part of the Amazon jigsaw to create a smart home and have a regular touch point with their customers. Alexa emerged from the kintsugi mindset, reframing mistakes as opportunities. Alexa appeared on the Amazon product suite one day, seemingly out of nowhere. As we know, Amazon had been building those core capabilities quietly over many years. Even if the capabilities did not materialise as Amazon expected, they were used to power a new product. This is what I call return on capability, which we will explore in Chapter Five. There are always assets in the ashes, when you add the lens of kintsugi thinking, you will spot them.

Chapter Two Takeaways

- Kintsugi thinking means reframing mistakes as learning opportunities.
- Mistakes are only failures when we don't learn from them.

- By reframing our approach to mistakes, we can fail our way to success.
- The more we expose ourselves to making mistakes in the pursuit of progress, the more opportunity we give ourselves to learn.
- How we react to failure has an immense impact on others, from a parent's reaction to a child's mistake to the leader of one of the most successful organisations of all time.
- Jeff Bezos' reaction to the Fire failure spoke volumes about the organisational mindset and encouraged further experimentation.
- When we embrace mistakes as learning outcomes, we can uncover new capabilities, new innovations and new opportunities.
- It is key to remember there are always assets in the ashes.

Considerations

For the individual

- How do you approach personal mistakes?
- Do you become defensive? If yes, why? If not, why? Trace the origins.
- Do you dissect the mistake to uncover the lesson?
- Do you see mistakes as an inevitable part of learning and discovery?
- How do you react to mistake to those you lead: as a manager, as a parent, as a peer?
- Do you have assets in your ashes?

For the organisation

- Do you permit mistakes when your team is experimenting?
- Does your team hide mistakes? If no, are you sure? If yes, why?

- How do you react when a mistake happens?
- Do you have permission to fail in the pursuit of innovation?
- Do you have assets in your ashes?
- Do you make it explicit that mistakes and innovation are symbiotic?
- Decide how you will approach mistakes in the future.
- As an organisation, set the parameters on mistakes, agree when they are tolerated and when they are not.
- Celebrate when a mistake is made in an attempt to achieve a lofty goal.
- Can you see how there are assets in the ashes?

3

S Curves: A Framework for Permanent Reinvention

'There is nothing in a caterpillar that tells you it's going to be a butterfly.'

—R. Buckminster Fuller

Imagine you live in the late 1890s, most people travel by horse-driven coach, railway and streetcar. Rail is more comfortable than horse and cart because roads are glorified dirt tracks and suspension is not yet widespread. When you hear rumours of this thing called a motorcar, 'a mechanical horse', you dismiss it as a passing craze. After a while, you see several motor cars appear. These first cars are unreliable, need a lot of maintenance and smell so badly that people call them 'stink chariots'. Besides all that, there are no roads on which to drive stink chariots.

This is a flavour of the environment in which Henry Ford pursued his vision of a high-quality car at an affordable price. Many obstacles stood in the way of that vision, trust in cars, the transport ecosystem and even securing investment in his company. Take for example, Horace Rackham, one of the early investors in The Ford Motor Company. With great uncertainty and

ALWAYS LOOKS LIKE
A STEP BACKWARDS

Figure 3.1 A faster horse

against the advice of others, Rackham bought fifty shares of Ford stock (from a total of eight hundred and ninety shares). The president of the Michigan Savings Bank strongly advised Rackham not to invest:[1] 'The horse is here to stay, but the automobile is only a novelty – a fad'. In retrospect, this seems like an awful prediction and perhaps we might even think we would never make such a mistake. However, we must consider the paradigm, the ecosystem and the prevailing conditions when such decisions are made. Let's look at it differently.

Consider the following questions. Do you foresee the widespread adoption of self-driving cars in the coming years? What about widespread drone delivery? And space travel? While these things are closer to becoming a reality today, several years ago they were considered science fiction; many people believe they still are.

Predicting the future presents a real challenge – it is difficult to see beyond that which currently exists. The difference between the 1900s and today is that technology, underpinned

---

[1] https://en.wikipedia.org/wiki/Horace_Rackham

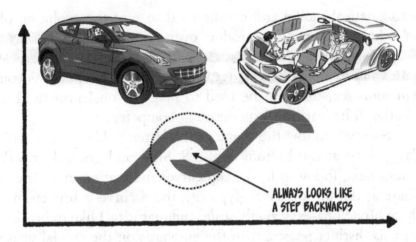

ALWAYS LOOKS LIKE
A STEP BACKWARDS

Figure 3.2   A jump too far?

by exponential speed, is galloping forward much faster than a mechanical horse ever could. This speed of change is why we need to update our mental models and frameworks to make sense of such phenomena. That is the goal of this chapter, to offer a simple framework, to reframe opportunities and threats so we can harness the winds of change.

S Curves

Many models of change exist, but one that is particularly relevant to disruptive innovation is the Sigmoid curve or S curve. Consider the S curve as a mental model or heuristic to frame a large variety of phenomena. We can think of the S curve as the optometrist's contraption, on which we can place new lenses, the lenses you will collect as you read through each chapter. Once you understand the S curve model, you can apply it to careers, business models and the arc of life itself.

Everett Rogers popularised the S curve in his book *Diffusion of Innovations*, first published in 1962. It stems from a mathematical model and can be used to plot the evolution of an industry, company or product over a period of time. S curve growth exhibits a progression from small beginnings that accelerates and approaches a climax, and eventually declines. As you will soon see, they can be used to map personal growth also, whether it be learning, experience or competency.

S curves follow the shape of the letter S, like a wave with flat growth at the bottom of the S. Slow and gradual growth comes next, followed by a steep curve culminating in a plateau phase at the top of the S. Typically, the S curve is broken into three broad phases: growth, scale, and maturity. I like to break it into six distinct phases, with the emphasis on the crucial phase six, which is often overlooked. This sixth phase is a blind spot, because it is counterintuitive; it also needs to begin before you reach phase five, but before we explore it, let's fully grasp the S curve model first.

Phase One

In phase one, we have a vision in its embryonic form. It may be a product in development or a new business model you ask your organisation to consider. As an individual, your vision may be a new career or a skill you want to develop. It is a great shame that

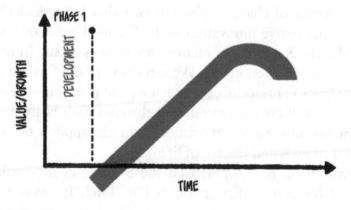

Figure 3.3   Phase One

many ideas do not even make it to this phase, because of our natural resistance to change. Like the caterpillar's immune system, sometimes it is you who quashes the idea. In organisations, it can be those who prefer things to stay as they are, the status quo. It can be hard to articulate an idea at this stage and even more difficult to garner support for a product or concept that never existed.

Phase Two

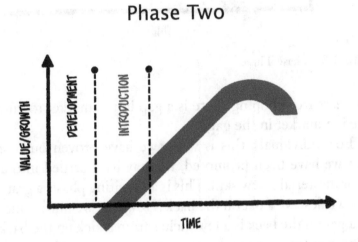

Figure 3.4   Phase Two

Phase two is when you have introduced your new product or service to the market. This is the trial-and-error phase, an adaptation phase as the market responds. As an individual, this phase may be the beginnings of a new career or hobby, or when you are still coming to grips with a new skill or role. This is a challenging phase; we often stumble here because the learning curve is steep. Our doubts, fears and vulnerabilities can get the better of us at this fragile point.

Phase Three

Phase three is when the market has responded positively to our new product or innovation and we can increase production. We have traction, we have lift off. This is the inflection point; we

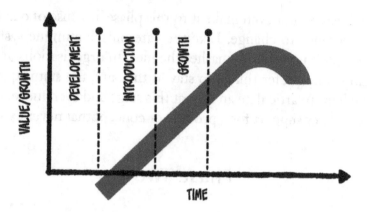

Figure 3.5   Phase Three

shift gears from hoping there is a gap in the market to knowing there is a market in the gap.

For individuals, this is when we have proven our competency, we have been promoted, we may have settled into a new role or mastered a new skill. This is an exciting phase, a gratifying one – we deserve a pat on the back. However, we must remember that a pat on the back is a few inches from a kick on the backside. It is here we can get caught in the success trap and become complacent, and that complacency is characteristic of the next phase.

Phase Four

'Celebrate your successes but forget them quickly, remember your losses more than your wins'.

—New Zealand Rugby Mantra

Phase four is a dangerous phase, when we have achieved success. We have established that our solution works, so we batten down the hatches to protect that success. We believe what has worked to get us here will continue to keep us there. Our successes can blind us to the possibility of failure, our victories can defeat us. We slide from an offensive mindset to a defensive one. Our hunger to go the extra mile to build a business or continually

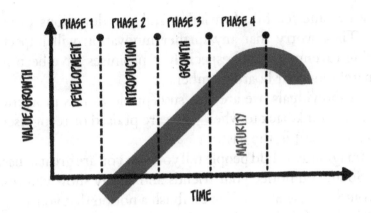

Figure 3.6 Phase Four

develop competence can be replaced by fear and defensiveness. Now we fear losing the success we have achieved and we focus on defending our competitive advantage. This defensive mindset blinds us to both threats and opportunities.

> *'It's easy to become dulled to danger when everything is working'.*
> —Whitney Johnson

In organisations, once a product delivers a predictable revenue stream, the organisational mindset shifts from experimenting with new products and business models to protecting established revenue. The business becomes blinded to the threat of disruption and new ways of doing things. For example, when a company first develops a new product, it is more willing to take small risks, because there is nothing to lose. This is an offensive mindset. However, when that product becomes successful and starts to deliver predictable revenue, the business capitalises on the success and defends the revenue stream. Often the innovation team who introduced the new revenue is pushed aside as if to say, 'let the adults take it from here'. This is particularly prevalent when an organisation is under revenue pressure and needs to fill the gap of revenue losses.

When the core organisation takes over emergent revenue streams, it often imposes unrealistic timelines on profitability.

They become fearful of mistakes and any deviations from the plan. They worry that any further innovation will impact the existing revenue stream, especially if promises have been made to shareholders or board members.

As individuals, we are also susceptible to this protectionist mindset. Think back to when you were praised or recognised for an achievement in the past.

Imagine as a child people tell you that you are great at basketball. Soon, you notice your friends and family show you respect for your sporting ability. You establish a notion that you are great at basketball. While this is positive, you can become protective of your achievement. If you become defensive, you can stop learning and become fearful of losing what you have already achieved. If you change your winning formula, they might stop praising you. You resolve to stick to what you have done in the past and not deviate from that well-worn path.

Then one day, you notice that people begin praising your younger brother for his basketball skills and you become jealous. 'Hey, that's my sport, how dare he?' In time, your friends, who were less concerned about protecting their existing success, become as accomplished as you. Why? Well, they continued to experiment, not fearing failure, like the pottery class you read about in Chapter Two, who failed their way to success. Suddenly, you find yourself a victim of personal disruption. This disruption occurs in careers all the time and will accelerate at an ever-increasing rate.

When others consider us experts in our field, we can become defensive of our apparent expertise. While focussing on defending that expertise, we dismiss information and/or people who threaten our domain of competence in any way. 'Hey, that's my expertise, how dare they?' When we descend into this defensive mindset, we become closed to learning conceptually and physiologically. We close our minds to new information in case it threatens what we already know and when we are stressed, we do not learn effectively.

In this VUCA environment, expertise is more fleeting than ever before. In a world of abundant information, where data changes rapidly, we simply cannot know it all. To become undisruptable, we must recognise that our ideas are just hypotheses and our positions are only temporary. We are custodians of a role, so we cannot overidentify with any role. Gone are the days of sitting on the laurels of success, because disruption is the new normal. Even when we become king of the mountain and reach the top of the S, the mountain can suddenly become a molehill. We will explore this further when we map Nokia on the S curve in Chapter Twelve, 'Defeated by Victory'.

Phase Five

I hope this book helps us all avoid phase five in any realm. You don't want to experience this in business or any aspect of life. This phase is occurring at an ever-increasing and frequent rate. Remember that the life expectancy of corporations has plummeted in the past fifty years. For many executives, this disruption comes as a surprise; they don't see it coming, even though the writing was very clearly on the wall.

Phase five is where organisations and individuals stagnate, decline and decay. They compete on marketing spend rather than product innovation. They compete on price rather than demand. They facilitate price cuts through job automation, optimisation

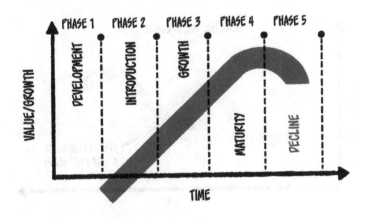

Figure 3.7   Phase Five

and 'me-too' propositions, where their products become generic. When threatened by start-ups and competitors, they resort to regulation and litigation rather than creativity and reinvention.

Phase five is a long kiss goodnight and a slow, painful decline where the organisation competes for an ever-decreasing market spend. This is the realm of the metaphorical melting iceberg. They are focussed on optimising for a world that no longer exists.

Individuals often suffer the same fate when they stop building new capability and depend solely on existing skills.

So, how do we avoid phase five and become undisruptable? The answer lies with phase six.

Phase Six: Jumping the S Curve

Phase six is 'jumping the S curve' and involves a transition from the success you have achieved today – whether it be in business or in your career – to possible success tomorrow. 'Well, that doesn't sound very certain', you may rightly think. It isn't; in fact, many S curve jumps don't yield expected or predictable results. Sometimes the output from an S curve jump is not a financial gain; it can often be a new capability or skill. If you are flexible, agile and adaptable to change, then this new capability can be applied to

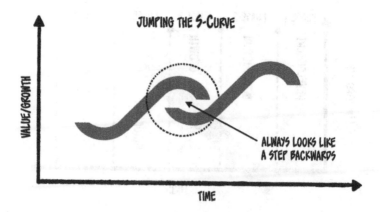

Figure 3.8 Jumping the S curve

another S curve. This is where we realise the value of 'kintsugi thinking'. Even if you don't succeed as you had predicted with your curve jump, you will certainly develop capability in your attempt. In a worst-case scenario, you discover what doesn't work, which brings you one step closer to what might work. With this mindset you see that both the wins and misses are rich with learning.

Return on Capability (RoC)

Do you remember Amazon's Fire Phone from the previous chapter? It was a financial mis-fire (ahem, couldn't resist), to the tune of $170m, but it yielded voice capability and eventually Alexa. This is what I call return on capability. Return on capability is the learnings, capabilities and mindsets you pick up when you jump the curve. So why don't more of us 'jump the S curve'?

Many individuals and organisations neglect this crucial phase because it is so damn counterintuitive. The jump to a new curve always looks like a step backwards. Next curve solutions are often immature, clunky and perform poorly compared to the existing offerings. This is what Buckminster Fuller meant when he said, "There is nothing in a caterpillar that tells you it's going to be a

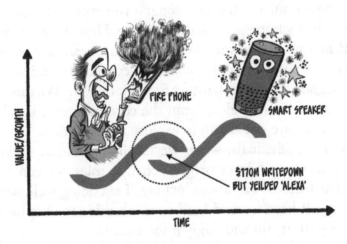

Figure 3.9   Return on capability

butterfly." An emergent idea often looks far different than the final product. As mentioned in the introduction, this is Amara's law in action, where we tend to overestimate the effect of a technology in the short run and underestimate the effect in the long run. Think how poorly Alexa or Siri performed when you first tried them. When Alexa launched in 2015, she had less than 100 skills. Today, Alexa skills have grown exponentially. The company claims that Alexa skills surpassed 100,000 worldwide by the end of 2020. There are now more than 100,000 skills available in the Alexa Skills store.

Think back to the first iPhone: it was a poor performer in terms of call quality, battery life, and network usage compared to existing mobile phone solutions such as Nokia handsets or the BlackBerry. Think back to when you started your career compared to your competence now. Think back to the motorcar versus the horse and cart.

With this context, imagine now that you are in charge of a large organisation. Your status, your compensation and your success rides on the successful exploitation of your current curve. This includes the achievement of quarterly targets and successful return on investment for your shareholders. Along comes one of your senior team, to present the concept of a curve jump to a new business model or new venture. They insist we must explore new business models while exploiting the existing ones. In fact, in a VUCA environment, they now suggest you explore a second curve before you reach the peak of the first one. How do you react?

When changemakers in established organisations suggest deviations from the core business, the common reaction is 'Let's just wait and let our competitors figure it out', or 'We can't afford to take any resources away from the core business'. Established organisations are not set up to explore new curves.

As for individuals, when we listen to internal inklings to develop new capabilities or even change roles, we can become defensive. Internal narratives include, 'I am doing well, why rock the boat?'. 'I have worked hard to climb this career ladder, I am just going to sit still and enjoy it for a while'.

These scenarios present the classic innovator's dilemma, popularised by the late Clayton Christensen. Christensen suggested we invest in new products and/or new business models that often compete with our existing businesses. Even though this move gives us access to a new customer segment, it may threaten our existing product lines. In addition, it distracts us from our current focus. To make the challenge even greater, the potential market may initially offer much less financial return, if any. While it can yield capabilities, an organisation is often ill equipped to take advantage of those new skillsets or mindsets. Encouraged by due diligence, financial teams conclude that such a curve jump will not be profitable, and advise that we double down on our current expertise in our current market. And thus, the stage is set for phase 5, decline.

In a slower business environment, once you had established a competitive advantage, you could happily defend it. Competitors could not catch up as easily as they can today, and you could maintain your head start.

Today, however, there is more competition and that competition is more global than ever before. A blend of digitisation, access to technology and cheap capital empowers entrepreneurs to become a competitor quicker than at any other time in history.

So, how do we jump the curve?

Building Capability Before You Need It

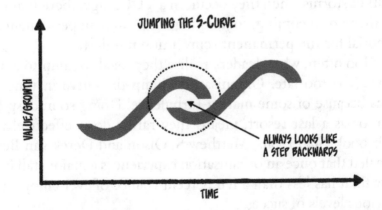

Figure 3.10   Jumping the S curve

'A corporation – essentially any institution – is a living, breathing organism made up of people, technology, institutional knowledge and relationships and is generally organized around mission and purpose. Entering into a crisis is not the time to figure out what you want to be. You must already be a well-functioning organization prepared to rapidly mobilize your resources, take your losses and survive another day for the good of all your stakeholders'.

—Jamie Dimon, Chairman and CEO JP Morgan

Look at Figure 3.10. Notice how the second curve starts long before we reach the peak of the first curve? We must initiate the second *as* we climb the first curve, not *when* we have exhausted the first one. When we experiment in times of abundance, we are more willing to accept mistakes in the pursuit of progress. We have the resources to support experimentation. This is what John F. Kennedy meant when he said, *'The time to repair the roof is when the sun is shining'*. This is the principle of the Spartan warrior mantra, 'The more you sweat in times of peace, the less you bleed in war'. This is the domain of the important, but not urgent. It is never urgent until it is. If we 'sweat in times of peace', it not only becomes part of our operational DNA, but it benefits us 'in times of war'. Just look at how many organisations have been caught out in this mid-pandemic world. Covid-19 accelerated the need for reinvention, digitisation and the adoption of remote working practices. The organisations who had repaired the roof when the sun was shining can weather storms when they occur. In a VUCA age, there is always another storm coming, so jumping the S curve in permanence is essential for the permanent reinvention mindset.

Too often, when leaders realise they need to jump to a new curve, it is too late. Organisations jump the curve in times of crisis because of some market turbulence. Doing so in desperation, or as a last resort, means they rarely do it effectively. In their book, *Stall Points*, Matthew S. Olson and Derek van Bever revealed that once an organisation experiences a major stall in its growth, it has less than a ten percent chance of ever enjoying its previous levels of success.

As for individuals, disruption might manifest as a sudden job loss when they find themselves on the wrong side of an organisational restructure. These are the moments when we regret that we did not use our time wisely. If only we had built new skills before they became mission critical.

In times of stress, fear or anxiety, the part of our brain responsible for rational thinking, the prefrontal cortex, shuts down. Our ability to innovate and make rational decisions is negatively impacted and we literally cannot think straight. This is another reason to build capabilities required for the next curve well before we need them.

This is why we see organisations once king of the hill like BlackBerry disrupted by Apple (more on that in Chapter Twelve). This is why we see the devastation of the media industry. This is why we see the retail apocalypse. This is why we will increasingly see the impact of artificial intelligence and algorithms on jobs in the future.

We will bring S curves to life in Part 3 where we will explore the S curve in action. We will see how some organisations became blinded by their success and stopped evolving. We will celebrate organisations and individuals who never stopped reinventing and adding new capabilities, long before they ever needed them.

Before we add further lenses to the permanent reinvention mindset, there is an important question to ask. With the speed of change so rapid, when is the right time to jump to the next curve, how do we know when to reinvent? The answer to that question is one of the anchors of this book: you never know when to jump to a new S curve, so you must do so in permanence.

If that is the case, then the S curve model itself must be reinvented. A slight tweak perhaps, an update to the model Everett Rogers popularised in the 1960s. In the next chapter, we will explore that update, the symbol of permanent reinvention: the infinity curve.

Chapter Three Takeaways

- The S curve is a mental model or heuristic to plot a large variety of phenomena: technology, business models and careers for example.
- The S curve is a fundamental model for a permanent reinvention mindset; think of it as the optometrist's contraption on which we can place the lenses you pick up in this book and beyond.
- S curve growth exhibits a progression from small beginnings that accelerate, approach a climax and eventually decline.
- The key phase comes in jumping to a new S curve.
- Jumping to a new S curve presents a plethora of challenges, the emergent idea often looks far different than the final product.
- Crucially, we must jump to a new S curve before it becomes necessary.
- When you jump to a new curve in desperation, your decision-making is flawed and you make poor choices.
- The key is to develop capabilities before you need them; this counts for individuals as well as organisations.
- Sometimes when you jump to a new curve, the results are not financial, they are what I call return on capability or RoC.
- RoC includes skills learned in the endeavour, mindsets established from the experiment and technology built from your efforts.

Considerations

For the individual

- Plot some major changes in your life on a series of two S-curves as you jumped from one curve to the next.

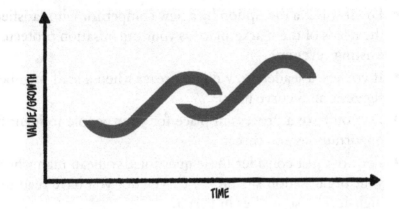

Figure 3.11   S curve jump

- Once complete, reflect on how you transitioned to the second curve.
- Did you wait until you had exhausted the first curve?
- Did you make a decision to jump curves after some setback like career stagnation?
- Did you make the leap before you needed to?
- Had you built capability in some other endeavour that came in useful in a future one?

For now, just consider these questions.
We will revisit them when we have the context of the examples from Part 3.

For the organisation

- Do you work in or have you worked in an organisation which did not jump to a new curve when it had the opportunity?
- Did the organisation suffer disruption by ignoring the opportunity?
- Did the organisation see the S curve jump as a step back?

- Did it suffer a disruption by a new competitor who satisfied the needs of the marketplace as your organisation protected existing revenue?
- If you are a leader, how do you react when a staff member suggests an S curve jump?
- Do you have a process in place for your people to identify opportunities and threats?
- For now, just consider these questions, you can map where your organisation sits on the curve after you have read the high-level case studies in Part 3.

4

The Ouroboros: Infinity Curve

'Out of perfection nothing can be made. Every process involves breaking something up. The earth must be broken to bring forth life. If the seed does not die there is no plant. Bread results from the death of wheat. Life lives on lives. Our own life lives on the acts of other people. If you are lifeworthy, you can take it'.

—Joseph Campbell

One night I had a disturbing dream of a snake swallowing its own tail. Whenever I have a dream or idea, I send them to an email address I keep solely for ideas. Several days later, I checked this 'ideas inbox' and one subject line jumped out amidst the rest. 'Snake swallowing own tail', it read. After several seconds, it came back to me, 'Oh yeah, what was that about?', I pondered. When I researched what it could possibly mean, I was buzzing with excitement. I had dreamed a perfect symbol to represent the permanent reinvention mindset. What's more, this symbol fits perfectly with the S curve, before I describe how, let's first explore the symbol known as the ouroboros.

The ouroboros is an ancient symbol often represented by a serpent or dragon eating its own tail. The ouroboros features in many ancient civilisations, including Egypt, Greece and Norse mythology. The word ouroboros originates from Greek and means 'tail eater' or 'tail devourer'. Many of us consider the snake to be a symbol of evil, but the ouroboros is actually a symbol for eternal, cyclical renewal or a cycle of life, death and rebirth. Psychiatrist Carl Jung considered the ouroboros as a symbol of immortality because by slaying himself, he brings himself to life. That definition reminded me of the butterfly who starts life as a caterpillar by devouring its own egg shell and then as a butterfly, it uses the caterpillar as fuel for its next becoming.

The ouroboros provides a lens through which we can reframe our approach to business and life. Using this lens, we can consider our former selves as fuel for our next reinvention.

Once we begin to establish a level of competence in any field, we must invest in ourselves ahead of the necessity to do so. We do this by unlearning what no longer serves us and learning what might serve us in the future. We do this particularly in VUCA times when success is fleeting. As author Eric Hoffer recognised, 'In times of profound change, the learners inherit the earth, while the learned find themselves beautifully equipped to deal with a world that no longer exists'.

Many organisations stop learning when they reach the top of their S curve. As soon as we reach the peak in any endeavour, the dip is already under way. In the late eighteenth century William Pollard recognised this when he said, 'Learning and innovation go hand in hand. The arrogance of success is to think that what you did yesterday will be sufficient for tomorrow'. You can see how the ouroboros is such a fitting symbol for reinvention, because it suggest a never-ending cycle of change, but it gets better. The serendipity of dreaming about this symbol struck me even more so when I saw what it looked like. It was the symbol of infinity, a perpetual loop. (See Figure 4.1).

A few days later, as I prepared my slides for a workshop, I noticed a pattern. Equipped with my new ouroboros lens, I realised there was a flaw in my mental model of S curve jumps.

THE OUROBOROS

Figure 4.1   The ouroboros

Until that moment, I had envisaged each S curve jump as the decline and death of the previous curve. Today, I realise that is fundamentally flawed. Each curve does not die, but fuels the next one. The curves are not isolated moments in time, they are arrested moments in a dynamic, plastic and perpetual process. This radically changes the concept of the S curve from a periodic jump to a permanent cycle, from an occasional transformation to a permanent reinvention.

AN ARRESTED MOMENT IN TIME

Figure 4.2   An arrested moment in time

As I stared at the image of the S Curve jumps in front of me (Figure 4.2) I felt something was missing. I picked up my pen and doubled the first S back upon itself, like the ouroboros devouring its tail. I couldn't believe I hadn't seen it before. Look what happens:

THE INFINITY CURVE

Figure 4.3   The infinity curve

In one of the many moments of serendipity that occurred while writing this book, this was top of the list. Behold the infinity curve, the symbol of permanent reinvention (Figure 4.3) and an S curve jump of the S curve model.

Why the Infinity Curve?

In the past, finding a killer product or establishing yourself in a career was a safe bet, but the world has changed dramatically. It is no longer enough to jump to a new curve when we feel the gales of disruption at our heels or when we experience stagnation and even decline. Instead, we must jump curves permanently. It is no longer a step in the process, it is now the very process itself.

This will require a shift in mindset for organisational leaders, shareholders, financiers, entrepreneurs and society as a whole. Organisations will need to seek new opportunities while exploiting existing ones. This means the new and the old curves work in harmony, merging as one. Each curve contributes to the other in a reciprocal relationship. For example, if the new curve requires existing resources, such as supply chain, funding or marketing, it can depend on the legacy organisation to deliver. The emergent curve reciprocates by delivering new business models, products, services, skillsets and mindsets. They are no longer separate entities: they are one, part of the same dynamic process.

This is not new; this is the very essence of life, it has been the way of the universe since life began. A tree does not die each year, it cycles through various stages of growth. When its leaves fall, they become fuel to nourish the roots; the tree stores that energy so that it can enjoy a future season of growth. Like the ouroboros, there is a constant cycle of dying and becoming.

When I was a child, I grew up in the Phoenix Park in Dublin, Ireland. My father was responsible for the Park. On one occasion he orchestrated the replanting of trees on the main avenue. He initiated that replanting project over twenty years ago and today those trees stand as fine specimens as the older ones age. Which reminds me of the Chinese saying, which is useful for those of us who think we have left it to late to take action. "The best time to plant a tree was twenty years ago. The second best time is now." In the context of permanent reinvention, this means that if you want success and growth in the future, the best time to act is now. He explained to me how they plant younger trees in the shade of older ones, because the older trees protect the young saplings. Some tree species (cottonwoods, aspens, poplars, pines) are rhizomatous, so that each new tree is actually part of the other trees and they are connected at the roots. To us, they appear to be separate trunks, but they are part of a deeply connected network. Organisations can take great lessons from nature, because they too are living organisms. An established organisation can shelter an emergent one until it can stand alone.

At an individual level, each of us must reframe our relationship with change, seeing it as an opportunity rather than a threat. We must infuse perpetual learning into our lives at work and at home. Perhaps organisations might move to a four-day week, allowing the fifth day as a learning day? We must allocate time to nurture new capabilities, skill sets and mindsets. Founder and CEO Emeritus of Visa, Dee Hock, put it this way, 'Life is eternal, perpetual becoming, or it is nothing. Becoming is not a thing to be known, commanded, or controlled. It is a magnificent, mysterious odyssey to be experienced'. Dee explained to me the difference between an odyssey and a journey. When you set out on a journey, you have a destination in mind. When you set out on an odyssey, it is for the joy of the adventure. I like this as a mental model for life and for organisational and career life cycles – there is no destination, it is always an odyssey.

However, if we are to embrace such mental shifts, then we need to reframe other outdated mental models. One of which is how we perceive time itself. Let's explore that next.

Chapter Four Takeaways

- The ouroboros is an ancient symbol for eternal, cyclical renewal or a cycle of life, death and rebirth.
- The ouroboros provides a perfect analogy for the reinvention of the S curve model.
- S curves are not isolated moments in time, but part of a perpetual process.
- When the S doubles back upon itself, it mirrors the ouroboros and reflects the concept of the caterpillar eating its own egg to fuel its future.
- Organisations can learn from this principle and see how the legacy organisation can fuel the emergent one.
- Individuals can use this as a mental model to reframe personal development as a perpetual odyssey.
- Unlike a journey, an odyssey has no fixed destination: permanent reinvention is an odyssey with no destination.

Considerations

For the individual

- Think of how skills and capabilities you developed in the past have fuelled you in ways you had never considered before.
- Are you still planting seeds for your future self?
- If your future self appeared to you today, what would they ask you to do?

For the organisation

- Do you see new iterations of the business as separate entities?
- How can you bring them closer together?
- Do you see the present business as fuel for the future?
- If you do not own the business you run and it was your business, what seeds would you plant for the future?

5

Recalibrating Time

Figure 5.1   The mayfly and the sequoia

'Life isn't a linear journey. Sometimes it's one step back-
wards, two steps forward and then a jump out to the side'.
                                                    —Karina Halle

A mayfly lives for only two days, while a sequoia tree lives for over one thousand years. Imagine you saw a mayfly resting on the branch of a sequoia tree and you asked that mayfly, 'Do you perceive this branch that you are standing on as being alive?' The mayfly would say, 'Of course not. I've been here my entire life and the branch hasn't done a thing'.

The Earth is like the tree and we are like the mayfly. We stand on a planet that was born four and a half billion years ago. While little seems to change during our lifetimes, a lot changes for the planet. Africa was once connected to the USA and Morocco to Cape Cod. Imagine for a moment, you were a different lifeform, sitting on the moon and looking down on Earth. If you blinked your eyes once every million years, you would see the planet blossoming to life.

I share this story to emphasise how everything on the planet evolves at a different rate. In the context of permanent reinvention, it is important to see that various aspects of our lives also develop at different speeds. We can't force the same timeline on everything, it only results in frustration and desperation. Our careers, our children, our relationships, our hobbies, our projects and our organisations all march to a different beat of time. The lens through which we perceive time has an enormous impact on how we experience the world.

In my workshops, I ask clients to plot their lives and the lives of their organisations. Without telling them why, I ask them to mark what age they believe to be the end of life and to mark with an X where they are today. On average people write eighty-five for their own lives. They guess that their organisation will survive maybe two hundred years. One hundred percent of the time, they draw some variation of the following illustration: a line from left to right.

Figure 5.2   A linear life

In Western traditions, we think of time in terms of past, present and future. The arrow of time moves from left to right: we are born, we live, we die. By contrast, Eastern philosophies view time as cyclical, everything is forever evolving. For many ancient cultures there is only one term to describe both the very deep past and the far distant future. This suggests that they see time as part of one cycle: a cyclical metamorphosis of the past into the future, like the ouroboros. The Inuit of Baffin Island, for example, use the term *uvatiarru* to convey both 'long ago' and 'in the future'. This perception of time is core to the permanent reinvention mindset. When we visualise time as a series of cycles, we reframe past experiences as fuel for the future, setbacks as lessons and sunk costs as learning costs. We are also more patient with our experiments as we uncover the future.

Using cyclical time as a lens helps us to reframe a variety of phenomena. A career can be in the equivalent of spring as you embark on a new one or in winter as you end another. Relationships may spend some time in autumn or winter. When you have children, they become the focus of your energy, they become your spring. Just because your relationship may experience an autumn does not mean it is over, it is just at a different stage of its perpetual life cycle. This can be difficult to fathom if you see your relationship as linear. When you reframe your relationship as cyclical, you realise, things will come back to normal if you are patient and continue to nurture it. Many animals hibernate to survive the harsh conditions of winter. While they rest, they stockpile energy to thrive once again in spring. Deciduous trees shed their leaves to conserve water and energy in the autumn. What appears to be a stressful time is just part of an ongoing cycle during which trees reabsorb valuable nutrients from their leaves and store them for later use in their roots. The tree uses the winter period to blossom again in spring.

I find this a useful way to perceive various aspects of life. Our lives are made up of a portfolio of seasons, a kaleidoscope of simultaneous evolutions, each at a different stage of its life cycle. If some aspect of our life is in bleak winter, perhaps it requires us to invest our energy so that it can enjoy spring.

As an organisation, this cyclical mindset provides a useful way to view transformation and reinvention efforts. When we reframe the organisation as a living entity, we see that it is also in a continual process of becoming. It also means that different aspects of the future evolve at various rates. Jeff Bezos is a proponent of thinking long and says of Amazon, 'We like things to work in five to seven years. We're willing to plant seeds, let them grow and we're very stubborn. We say we're stubborn on vision and flexible on details'.

Figure 5.3   Linear life cycle

Before we continue, compare the illustration of a linear life cycle above (Figure 5.3) to the cyclical one below.

In this illustration (Figure 5.4), notice how each life experience is reframed as fuel for the next. Just like the butterfly, we use our former self to fuel the next. Lao Tzu said, 'Life is a series of natural and spontaneous changes. Don't resist them; that only creates sorrow. Let reality be reality. Let things flow naturally forward in whatever way they like'. Perceiving life in a cyclical way helps us to enjoy the cycles, but also to let them go.

Figure 5.4   Cyclical life

When things don't work out as planned, we still gain valuable lessons. We understand there are assets in the ashes. Business leaders can reframe reinvention as a process of building on the past, rather than defending it. Linear mindsets assume what worked yesterday will work today and what worked today will work tomorrow. By now, we have established that is not the case.

With a clear understanding of S curves and infinity curves, we can now use these mental models to add further lenses. Part 2 introduces a variety of lenses that will culminate with the permanent reinvention mindset. Let's start where every new idea, every new business and every reinvention begins: vision.

Chapter Five Takeaways

- We have been conditioned to think of time as linear.
- Ancient cultures perceived time as cyclical.
- Cyclical time works perfectly for the concept of the infinity curve; cycles suggest there is no end, just the beginning of the next cycle.
- Cycles are a great way to reframe every aspect of your life, from your career to your relationship, each interacting with the other and each at a different stage of its own life cycle.

Considerations

For the individual

- Using Figure 5.5 as a guide, plot your life in a linear mode.
- Draw an X where you are today.
- Draw a √ to represent major events in your lifeline: college, jobs, hobbies, relationships, etc.
- Next, using Figure 5.6 as a guide, plot your life as a series of cycles.
- Notice how each cycle contains some valuable skills or experiences that are useful for a future cycle: like the caterpillar to the butterfly, you use your former self as fuel for the next.
- This is a useful mindset when considering your career, where one role can impart valuable skills that you build upon in another.

Figure 5.5   Linear life plot exercise

Figure 5.6   Cyclical life plot exercise

- Think of your hobbies and interests in the same way; perhaps those art lessons you took gave you a unique way to interpret data? Innovation happens at the intersections, so the more areas that intersect, the more unique your view.

For the organisation

- Consider how you measure success.
- Consider for a moment the exploratory projects that your people are working on.
- Plot them in a linear mode.
- Notice how it leaves no room for learning.
- Learning and innovation are symbiotic, we must create space for people to learn.
- Every learning curve exposes a weakness, but with each iteration mistakes will happen, which is essential for success to emerge.
- Now plot projects in a cyclical manner, where each phase results in an outcome.
- Sometimes the output will not meet expectations.
- Each time an outcome does not match our assumptions, it pushes us in a more fruitful direction.
- Look for return on capability, which includes mindset, skills and even technologies that may be useful in future endeavours. There are always assets in the ashes.
- Be patient with your transformation efforts; they take time, it is a ripple and not a splash.
- For change to happen, you will go through cycles; perhaps your organisation will need to experience a winter so that it can enjoy a spring.

PART 2

Permanent Reinvention Lenses

6

The Wasp Trap: Personal Vision

WHAT HARM COULD IT DO?

Figure 6.1   The wasp trap

'Where there is no vision, the people perish'.
　　　　　　　　　　　　　　　　—Proverbs 29:18

It was our summer holiday and we had rented a cabin in a
pine forest in the Irish countryside. There was a queue of cars to

check in, so we waited with windows down, enjoying the fresh country air. Suddenly there was a ruckus in the back of the car, a wasp had lunged at my son's ice cream. When the wasp fled our wild thrashing, my son asked why wasps attack at the end of the summer. I had never thought about it before, but we decided to find out. Our 'cabin research' revealed the answer lies in the fascinating life cycle of the wasp colony. I also uncovered a great analogy for purpose and vision.

In spring, a fertilised queen emerges from hibernation and looks for food. Insect skeletons are made from chitin, a material made from tightly bound sugars. To sustain chitin, she needs sweet liquids that contain high-energy sugars. At this stage of life, queen wasps get their sugar from flowers and by licking the sugar water from bees. This behaviour changes after she builds a nest and lays eggs. As many working parents know, you are often so busy tending to the needs of your infants that you don't have time to look after yourself. The queen wasp is no different. She is so busy building the colony and hunting food for her larvae that she doesn't have time to feed herself. Unlike humans, wasps deal with this challenge in a remarkable way.

Because grubs need protein to grow, the queen hunts insects. When she feeds these chewed up insects to the grubs, they convert the chitin from the insects into simple sugars and feed this to the queen. This allows the queen to focus on the all-important task of growing the colony rather than hunting food for herself. When the grubs develop into sterile female workers, they take over the feeding duties. The worker wasps don't waste time feeding themselves either, so the larvae feed them with the same sugary substance, once they bring them chewed-up chitin.

This life cycle continues until late summer, when everything changes. The queen stops producing worker wasps and instead produces new queens and male wasps to fertilise those queens. The fertilised females become new queens and hibernate in cocoons until the forthcoming spring, when those that have survived the winter begin the next cycle. Now, that's all great for the survival of the species, but what about all those workers?

When the colony reaches its peak, the queen stops releasing a pheromone that maintained colony cohesion. Without this unifying pheromone the colony rapidly disintegrates. With no more larvae to convert chitin into sugars and an increasing shortage of food, worker wasps have no choice but to seek their sugar fix elsewhere. Desperate to feed, foraging worker wasps now take more aggressive risks. This is why picnics, lollipops and dumpsters are so appealing.

I share this story to emphasise that, without a uniting purpose, the wasps wander aimlessly. This is what I call the *W.A.S.P. Trap*, **W.**andering **A.**imlessly **S.**ans **P.**urpose. Wasp life cycles are shorter than ours, but the W.A.S.P. trap highlights why purpose is so important. Without something to strive for, without a vision, we wander aimlessly through life. This chapter focuses on personal vision, while the next explores organisational vision.

Where There Is No Vision, the People Perish

Proverbs 29:18 reads, '*Where there is no vision, the people perish*'. The Hebrew word for perish is *paw-rah*. Paw-rah refers to the headdress that prevents a woman's hair from blowing directionless in the wind. This reminds me of the wasp colony and how, in the absence of the uniting pheromone, the worker wasps were left without direction. We are all liable to wander through life. We all need a purpose, and purpose begins with having a vision.

Figure 6.2   Vision lives on top of the S curve

Vision is a crucial requirement for the reinvention mindset, it is the first step in any transformation.

Vision lives at the top the S Curve and serves as a North Star to guide us. If we imagine the top of the curve as a mountain to climb, vision is what we imagine it will look like when we get there. It doesn't matter if that vision is fuzzy and not fully formed, it provides a magnetic force to draw us through the inevitable obstacles and setbacks we encounter on the way up any curve.

Many of us only realise that we lack a vision and purpose when we encounter a crisis. Some of us experienced this during the Covid-19 pandemic and ensuing economic downturn, which, at the time of writing (December 2020), is in full force. We binge on Netflix, social media and a variety of substances. Sometimes we even hover around the fridge like a wasp around a dumpster. Before the lockdown, the busyness of life – with work, school runs and various errands – blinded us to our lack of vision and purpose.

Vision informs purpose. Just as we need to build capability before we need it, we need to cultivate vison in our lives before we discover we have none. If we don't have a vision for each curve of our lives, what does it mean when one curve declines? Let's explore the example of retirement.

Retirement

'There is no joy to be had from retirement, except in some kind of productive work. Otherwise, you degenerate into talking to everybody about your pains and pills. The point is not to retire from work or you will shrivel up into a nuisance to all mankind'.

— Herbert Hoover

While worker wasps die soon after the colony degenerates, we have lots of life left in the tank when our working lives end. Unfortunately, many of us do not cultivate a vision for retirement, leaving many people bereft of meaning when they retire. Confronted with the abrupt realisation that they overidentified with their careers, they wander aimlessly like the late-summer wasp. Research reveals a two percent increase in male mortality immediately after age sixty-two. The rise is directly related to retirement, with the mortality rate increasing among those who stop working because social security becomes available.

It doesn't have to be this way. The Japanese have a term for turning sixty. They call it 'The Kanreki' and consider it a rebirth. The word 'Kanreki' derives its meaning from the words kan (return) and reki (calendar). Therefore, turning sixty is viewed as your chance to start over again, a new cycle to enjoy.

Retirement from a sporting career confers many gifts. A major gift I received is that life comes in cycles. Careers are like S curves, you eventually plateau, especially if you do not reinvent before it becomes urgent. Unlike organisations, which cannot gauge when they have reached the peak of their curve, we know when we reach the top of our career curve. Retirement offers the opportunity to use some of the capabilities we have built over a lifetime. Entering retirement with a vision and purpose has a significant impact on those years.

Having a vision for any stage of life is essential. It helps you live a more fulfilled life, one with minimal regrets. Once you commit to a vision, the most amazing things happen in a phenomenon called synchronicity.

Living in Synchronicity

'Until one is committed, there is hesitancy, the chance to draw back, always ineffectiveness. Concerning all acts of initiative (and creation), there is one elementary truth, the ignorance of which kills countless ideas and splendid plans: that the moment one definitely commits oneself, then Providence moves too. All sorts of things occur to help one that would never otherwise have occurred. A whole stream of events issues from the decision, raising in one's favour all manner of unforeseen incidents and meetings and material assistance, which no man could have dreamt would have come his way. I have learned a deep respect for one of Goethe's couplets: "Whatever you can do, or dream you can, begin it. Boldness has genius, power, and magic in it!"'

—William Hutchison Murray

The psychologist Carl Jung used the term synchronicity to describe 'meaningful coincidences' in life. Jung believed that, just as events may be connected by causality, they may also be connected by meaning. Vision informs meaning and is symbiotic with purpose. Once we commit to a vision, once we decide on a purpose, we have a heightened awareness of opportunities and synchronicities that we may otherwise have overlooked. Without a clear vision, we don't have our radar on for opportunities that are often sitting right in front of us. Having a vision sets the wheels of synchronicity in motion. Then it becomes a virtuous cycle: the more opportunities you seize, the closer you come towards achieving your vision and the more you are encouraged. Such thinking can be dismissed as new-age mumbo jumbo, and perhaps it is synchronicity in action, but there just happens to be a physiological reason that explains why it works.

The RAS: The Science of Synchronicity

'We shape our life by deciding to pay attention to it. It is the direction of our attention and its intensity that determines what we accomplish and how well'.

—Mihaly Csikszentmihalyi

In the base of our brains, we have an information filtering system called the reticular activating system, the RAS, which consists of a series of neural networks. A primary function of the RAS is to filter information that we deem important for our survival. When we consistently invoke a clear vision of what we want to achieve, when we mentally rehearse it, we activate the RAS. It is as if the RAS is a sniffer dog: once you give it a scent to track, the RAS gets to work.

We experience this phenomenon all the time. Let's say, for example, you want to buy a new car. You decide to buy a black Tesla. This is a car you had never seen before you chose it in the dealership. But now, as if by magic, you see black Teslas everywhere. You told your brain what is important to you, so it looks for validation.

Figure 6.3 The RAS sniffer dog

I consider this to be the science behind the law of attraction, where we attract those things we focus on most. It is why positive people see reasons to be positive and why negative people find more reasons to be negative. It is why journaling changes how we think. Even when you spot the smallest reasons for which to be grateful, they gradually sculpt your brain to see more reasons to be grateful. It is why cultivating a permanent reinvention mindset will give you a higher likelihood of becoming undisruptable. Research shows that invoking your vision regularly has a dramatic impact on our results in any endeavour.

The Mind Gym

'If you can hold it in your head, you can hold it in your hand'.
—Bob Proctor

Perfect practice makes perfect, right? But does that practice have to be physical or could it be imagined? I was an average athlete, last picked in the playground and even throughout my adolescence. Visualising myself as a professional player had a dramatic outcome on my career. Every athlete will attest how effective this is. Their success started with a vision and they regularly visualised that vision as a fait accompli.

Maxwell Maltz was the pioneer of a field of psychological training called psycho-cybernetics. He believed that our nervous system cannot tell the difference between an imagined and a real experience. Our nervous systems react appropriately to what we think, or imagine, to be true. This means we can fool our brains into believing something has already happened. When we visualise an outcome, neurons in our brains fire and cognitively 'pave the way' for that future event, as long as we do the work required to achieve that desired outcome. Fascinating research shows how powerful such visualisation can be.

In 1996, Judd Blaslotto, of the University of Chicago, wanted to test the power of visualisation. The test went as follows.

He split basketball players into three random groups. He tested each group to measure how many points they scored with a limited number of free throws. In the lead-up to the test:

Group one was instructed not to touch a basketball.

Group two was instructed to practice free throws for one hour every day.

Group three simply visualised making free throws.

After thirty days, Blaslotto tested them again.

Group one showed no improvement, as you might expect.

Group two showed a twenty-four percent improvement.

Group three, who simply visualised making free throws, showed a twenty-three percent improvement.

In a related study, a Professor of Neurology at Harvard Medical School, Alvaro Pascual-Leone, divided volunteers into two groups. He gave Group One a five-finger piano exercise to practise every day for two hours, five days a week. After each session, he measured the neural activation of the group. He noticed that, even after just five days of practice, new neural circuits were had been established.

He asked the second group to imagine playing the same piano piece each day. When he measured this group, he found that with mental rehearsal alone this group had developed new neural connections just like group one had achieved with physical rehearsals.

After two weeks, the performances of the two groups were almost identical.

While these studies prove the science of visualisation, just ask any successful person if they have ever visualised their goals. The majority will say yes and many others actually do so, but have never realised it. Hard work is essential, but when we imagine, dream and cultivate a vision of what we want, we are far more likely to achieve it. Thoughts have power because thoughts are energy.

> 'I never hit a shot, even in practice, without having a very sharp, in focus picture of it in my head. It's like a color movie. First I "see" the ball where I want it to finish, nice and high and sitting up high on the bright green grass. Then the scene quickly changes and I "see" the ball going there: its path, trajectory, and shape, even its behaviour on landing'.
> —Jack Nicklaus, Golf My Way

While this chapter has focused on personal vision, let's now look at the importance of organisational vision. Like the queen wasp, who emits a unifying pheromone, organisations can align people around a compelling vison to achieve dramatic results. In 2020, Apple became the first company to be valued at two trillion dollars. It reached the milestone just two years after becoming the world's first trillion-dollar company in 2018. That success stems back to 2001, when Steve Jobs shared Apple's vision for the future. Let's look at organisational vision next.

Chapter Six Takeaways

- Vision is the magnetic force that compels us towards a new becoming.
- Even if our vision is blurry, it acts as a North Star to guide us.
- Without vision, we may think we are busy but might be wandering aimlessly without (sans) purpose.
- Studies show that many people rapidly decline after retirement, particularly if they have overidentified with their careers.
- This provides a warning shot for all of us to cultivate vision across all areas of our lives.
- Once you set a vision, you activate your RAS, the reticular activating system, a part of your brain that filters information that you deem important.
- The RAS is why many of us experience life so differently.
- When you have a vision, you become aware of all kinds of opportunities and serendipities that you may otherwise have overlooked.
- Studies show that, when we visualise, in addition to doing the required work we are far more likely to achieve success.

Considerations

For the individual

- Do you have a vision for the various phases of your life?
- Are you wandering aimlessly towards retirement?
- If you are retiring soon, what is your vision for your Kanreki?
- On the following S curve write a one-word vision for your current life stage; it could simply be to learn everything you can in your role, or perhaps be a great example for your niece, child, employees.

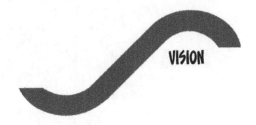

Figure 6.4   Vision Exercise 1

Figure 6.5   Vision Exercise 2

On the S curves above (Figure 6.5) plot your visions for various projects, hobbies, elements of your life.

For the organisation

- Do you encourage your people to cultivate a personal vision?
- As a team manager, do you encourage your team members to have personal visions for their roles?

7

All Roads Lead to Rome: Organisational Vision

Figure 7.1 Archimedes' death ray

'The sun's rays do not burn until brought to a focus'.
                                        —Alexander Graham Bell

During the siege of Syracuse in 212 BC, mathematician and inventor Archimedes allegedly constructed a death ray to destroy Roman warships. His contraption concentrated sunlight through a sequence of mirrors to create an intense beam that set enemy ships ablaze. Archimedes pretty much invented the first laser beam.

Normal light, such as sunlight, is incoherent or dispersed; thankfully it does not burn through things like a laser would. Lasers emit particles of light, known as photons. When photons are aligned in lockstep, they are described as 'coherent'. When light is tightly concentrated like a laser it is not only potent but can stay focused over vast distances. You can see where I am going with this, it provides a powerful analogy for organisational vision.

When leaders align human energy in a coherent way towards a common vision, our efforts are magnified. Sometimes, we mistakenly believe we are aligned. While a leadership team may be aligned, as you move down through the ranks of the organisation,

Figure 7.2   Octopus on rollerblades

the light becomes increasingly dispersed. As a result, many people appear to be busy, but are like an octopus on rollerblades – lots of movement but no direction. (See Figure 7.2)

They are like the worker wasps of the last chapter, wandering aimlessly. Just as queen wasps release unifying pheromones for their colony, a leader must share a unifying vision for their organisation. In the last chapter, we explored the importance of vision from a personal standpoint. In this chapter, we will examine the importance of vision for a group of people. We will see how Steve Jobs achieved amazing results by using the power of his vision to create the future. But first, let's explore how organisational vision works.

All Roads Lead to Rome

In pre-Roman times, roads were dirt tracks, twisting and turning as they encountered obstacles. The Romans were the first to pave

Figure 7.3   Roman hub and spoke

roads, making them usable in adverse weather conditions. They executed a vision of a vast network of roads that was central to the success of the Roman empire. This was a hub and spoke network: if you visualise the wheel of a bicycle, the spokes of the wheel converge on a central point, called the hub (see Figure 7.4).

Hub and spoke models are still used by transport planners, airlines and network developers. The Roman hub and spoke transport network ensured Rome became the centre of commerce, trade, politics, culture and military dominance in and around the Mediterranean. The roads represented the spokes that connected Rome to the places it ruled, conquered or would conquer in the future. This snapshot of Roman history shows how a vision, supported by execution, can ensure years of dominance, even if that dominance eventually ends. It also provides a useful mental model for how we can use visions of the future to shape the present.

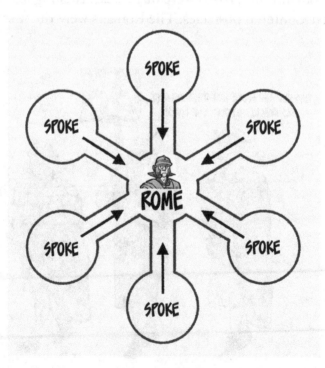

Figure 7.4   Roman hub and spoke network

Many of us associate the word *Abracadabra* with magicians pulling rabbits from hats, but it is an Aramaic term that translates into English as, 'I will create as I speak'. A clearly articulated vision works in a similar way: the words create a mental pathway to a future state.

In Chapter Six, the basketball study showed how visualisation creates neural pathways to a future skill, even when it has not been physically rehearsed. In a similar way, organisational leaders can pave mental roadmaps to a future goal by vividly and regularly articulating a vision. The more emotional and vivid the vision, the stronger the organisational neurons will fire and wire. Articulating a vision frequently provides mental rehearsal for employees, like the mental free throws for basketball players or mental recitals for pianists. Vision harnesses collective energy, just as Archimedes' death ray harnessed disparate beams of light into a laser beam. Collective vision does not just result in happy employees, but has an incredible impact on the bottom line, as Steve Jobs discovered to dramatic effect.

Apple and the Digital Hub

On January 9, 2001, Steve Jobs publicly unveiled Apple's vision of a digital hub. This vision has yielded incredible growth. In 2018, Apple became the world's first trillion-dollar company and became a two-trillion-dollar company only two years later.

Back in 2001, commentators speculated that the age of the personal computer was over. In a prophetic statement, Jobs announced that the PC was not dead, it had just evolved. His declaration heralded years of unprecedented growth that paved the way for Apple's success. That success owes a lot to the vision of a digital hub, a vision that united the organisation towards a common goal.

Jobs opened that seminal keynote with a question, 'What is our vision? A lot of people have come to ask that of our whole industry'. Then, with his competitors watching, he clearly outlined the vision that utterly transformed the industry.

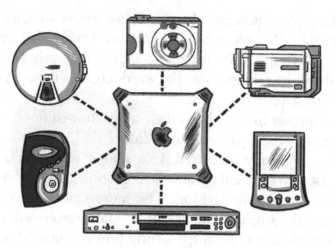

Figure 7.5 Apple's digital hub

At the turn of the millennium, consumer digital devices were everywhere. There were DVD players, digital cameras, CD players and their new cousin the mp3 player. They were stand-alone devices and most did not have any way to connect to the Internet. Think of these devices as disconnected territories that the Romans were yet to conquer. Apple needed a means to connect these disparate products. If they succeeded, Apple could become the Roman empire of the computing industry.

Just as the jump from horses to cars appears to be such an obvious one in retrospect, the jump to a digital hub makes perfect sense today. However, Jobs had to paint an incredibly vivid vision to rally his troops and to prime and excite his future customers. With a touch of abracadabra, his words were like a magician's wand, and his people delivered the vision. He presented the Mac computer as the hub, interconnected with any number of disparate digital devices. By announcing the 'Digital Hub', he inspired his company, consumers and even competitors. What Jobs didn't reveal was that Apple would not just produce the Mac as the central hub, but Apple would, in time, produce the spokes that connected to that hub. Apple's vision gave us the iPod, iTunes, Apple TV, Apple Music, iPhoto . . . and later iCloud, iPhone, iPad, iWatch, and ultimately a two-trillion dollar undisruptable organisation.

It is also important to realise that, in the noughties, Apple was like the wasp colony at the end of a cycle; it had experienced many challenges. Jobs had to streamline products and had to hire and fire to get the right people into the company and the wrong people out. It was only then that he announced his vision. Vision requires the right people to execute that vision.

A Vision and Execute Model

Just as the worker wasps of the colony need a unifying goal, employees also need purpose. When a group of people collect their efforts towards a common goal, results can be spectacular. In Figure 7.6, I exchange the central hub with a vision, then I invert the arrows coming from the execution back to the vision. Each spoke represents the diverse activities of your employees. People

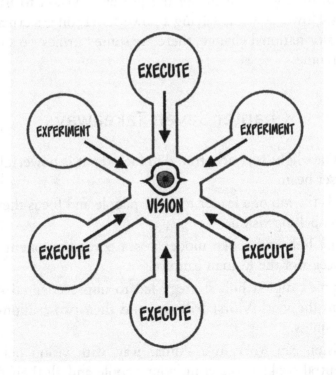

Figure 7.6 Vision and execute

will do a better job, and spot threats and opportunities, when they understand and are aligned with a vision. The speed of change is too rapid for leaders to spot all the trends and opportunities for their organisation; when employees are empowered by a vision, they can bring observations back to the hub and further inform the vision.

Notice how Figure 7.6 has some spokes reserved for experimentation. This is a key step in a VUCA age. Remember, we must experiment before it becomes necessary, it won't always yield financial gain but it may yield capability that can be used elsewhere. Jobs identified that the PC industry had reached a stall point in 2001 – eventually everything does. Jobs also identified that the key to success is to continually reinvent.

The Romans paved the way to the future by literally paving the way from that future back to Rome. Apple paved the way to their future with a powerful vision of the digital hub. In times of flux, we need to use the power of vision to pave our futures. However, while having a powerful vision is a crucial step in transformational change, there are some hurdles we still need to overcome.

Chapter Seven Takeaways

- When light is concentrated in lockstep it is powerful, like a laser beam.
- It is the job of a leader to unite people and focus them on a compelling vision.
- The hub and spoke model was a core component of the success of the Roman Empire.
- Apple's digital hub strategy led to unprecedented success and the world's first trillion-, and then two-trillion-dollar business.
- Vision can work in a similar way, with vision being the central spoke connecting your people and all their diverse activities.

- Without vision, your organisation may be busy, but disconnected, lots of movement but no direction, like an octopus on rollerblades.
- Articulating your vision publicly can also excite your future customers.

For the organisation

- Do your people know what your vision is?
- Do you articulate and update the vision regularly?
- Is the vision only clear with the leadership team but not throughout the organisation?
- Do you have a public-facing vision to excite customers?

Actions

- Create your vision statement but remember to include your people; they will be more committed when they are involved.
- Create a public vision and articulate it regularly; align anyone who speaks to the public so that the public hear a consistent message.

8

Managing Contrasts

'If we had no winter, the spring would not be so pleasant: if we did not sometimes taste of adversity, prosperity would not be so welcome.'

—Anne Bradstreet

One evening, as I prepared a bath for my sons, I ran my hand through the water to test the temperature. As I did, I observed the wave that I created. I called my sons to come and have a look. I asked them to watch the wave as I swished the water left and right. They looked at me the way they often do when I impart a lesson – with part tolerance, part amusement. I asked if they believed the bath contained just one body of water. Encouraged by their nodding heads, I demonstrated how even though it is the same body of water, it is both high and low at the same time. The wave has a crest and trough simultaneously.

'The water is like life', I said, 'the top of the wave represents the good experiences in our lives, and we must be grateful for and enjoy those times. But', I continued, 'just as we enjoy good experiences at the crest of the wave, we encounter bad days and disappointments in the trough. The secret is to manage the times at the bottom and enjoy the times at the top'. Lesson over,

I looked at my older son, who nodded in acknowledgment. As I turned to my younger son, his eyes remained fixed on the bobbing wave. Excitedly, he exclaimed, 'Will you put me in there and do that?' and so I did.

About a month later, my older son broke his arm in a fall from the trampoline. When I asked how he was, he replied, with a wry smile, 'I just managed the bottom of a wave'. To my heart's delight, the message of the waves had landed all those weeks earlier. That moment was certainly the crest of a wave for me and I took a moment to enjoy it.

A strange dynamic unfolds once we commit to a vision. While we experience a slew of serendipitous events that spur us on, we also encounter the exact opposite of what we desire. Every imaginable obstacle arises, every conceivable thought why we should stop comes to mind. This dynamic is common to every transformation journey: from changing careers to starting a new business, to reinventing a legacy organisation. The source of this duality is called the law of opposites. When you understand this law, you recognise when it occurs – you can even anticipate it. In doing so, you will see how the troughs signal that a crest is on its way. When we realise obstacles are a rite of passage on the journey towards success, we see them as milestones rather than millstones. When we encounter the things in life that we don't want, we appreciate even more the things we do. If our vision was easy to achieve, there would be no challenge, everyone would do it and no one would appreciate it.

According to the law of opposites, everything exists on a continuum. One phenomenon cannot exist without the potential for its opposite. For example, if you are reading this book as black text, then the background must be light to offer a contrast so you can distinguish the text. If you are reading on a digital device, perhaps the text is white, which means the background must be dark.

If you are stuck in your career, or have a boss you do not like, the law of opposites could be revealing what you do not want, so you can better understand what you do want. Sometimes we need to fail our way to success; the lessons stick better that way. Adding this lens to our mindset means we might now see S curves in a similar way.

S Curves as Opposites

'There is no gain without struggle.'
— Martin Luther King Jr.

When preparing the illustrations for this book, it struck me how the shape of a wave is similar to an S curve. The steep curve as you climb the wave represents the trough of challenges and the crest represents the success you enjoy when you reach the top. This is like the learning curve when we grasp a new skill or the hardships we encounter when developing a new product or the resistance we face when we reinvent an organisation.

In *Hardwiring Happiness*, neuropsychologist Rick Hanson explains that our brains are wired to rank the negative higher than the positive. Even when ten great things happen to us in a day, if we have one minor negative experience, we will focus on the solitary negative. This wiring stems back to our lives on the great savanna where we needed a negative bias in order to survive. Back then, we couldn't afford to second-guess if a rustle in the dark was a friendly animal or a man-eating cat, so we

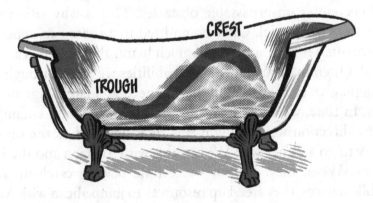

Figure 8.1   Trough and crest

erred on the side of the negative. A negative bias was essential then, and still is today if we encounter life-threatening situations. While the fear centre of our brains is always scanning for threats, our brains can misinterpret new experiences as threats. As a result, when we pursue a new vision, our brains will concoct every possible reason why we should avert the possible danger.

As soon as we meet an inevitable obstacle, we might wrongly interpret it to be a sign that it was not meant to be. By understanding the law of opposites, we can persevere through the difficult stages that arise during any odyssey. Without prior knowledge of the law of opposites, many dreams are unnecessarily lost or stillborn.

Difficulties come in a variety of forms. If we want to change career, sometimes it is our friends, partners and even parents who discourage us. The very people we expected to support us do not. You walk away from those moments thinking, 'I thought you were the one person I could count on to encourage me!' Don't be discouraged; most of the time, they are well-meaning and don't want to see you get hurt. They are also playing their role in the law of opposites, providing you with contrast. Someone will play that role; you can count on it. In any endeavour at least one person will discourage you, try to block you or hold you back. Instead of condemning them, realise that it is part of the process. However, even when we do receive abundant support, a multitude of problems still await.

Sometimes, even when we've done everything right, we still encounter unsurpassable obstacles. This is why vision and purpose are essential. Once committed to a vision, an apparent failure often reveals something much better than you had anticipated. Often the resilience and capabilities we learn through the struggle give us the strength we will need at a later stage in our lives. In time, we come to realise that not becoming entangled in the direction we'd thought was right afforded us the opportunity to go another way. We saw this with Amazon and the Fire Phone. When they did not waste time playing catch-up with mobile devices, they freed up resources to jump ahead with Alexa and other innovations. Of course, it is only in retrospect that we will realise by not becoming entangled in one direction we had time to go another way. As Steve Jobs said, 'You can't connect the dots looking forward; you can only connect them looking backwards. So you have to trust that the dots will somehow connect in your future. You have to trust in something – your gut, destiny, life, karma, whatever.'

This happened in my rugby career. When I was twenty-one, I set a vision to play for the champions of Europe, the French giants Toulouse. At that time, I didn't even have a professional contract in Ireland. I wasn't quite starting from zero, but I was only starting on the curve. I eventually signed a contract and enjoyed several years playing for my home club Leinster and eventually representing my country. That was the crest, but then came the trough.

After reaching one peak of playing for Ireland, everything that could go wrong did go wrong. I broke my arm, strained knee ligaments, pulled a hamstring and encountered a couple of years marred by injuries. When I wasn't injured, the coach rarely selected me. I couldn't seem to get out of the trough of the wave, but sometimes that is exactly the point. To get out of the trough of one wave, we need to jump to a new curve altogether.

I decided it was time to pursue my dormant vision to play in France. While it started out as a long shot, only a few months later I was in the starting team for Toulouse. I had achieved my vision. It wasn't easy, getting there was jammed with obstacles. When I first contacted an agent, a dozen clubs other than Toulouse offered me a contract. To my agent's frustration, I declined those offers politely until we got a meeting with Toulouse. While my time there was short, it was still the best thing I did in rugby: it wasn't so much that I played for the best team in Europe, it was that I had lived the experiences that I now share in this book. Setting a vision and then overcoming the obstacles that accompany any vision, experiencing contrasts, developing capabilities, overcoming resistance, these are all the ingredients of the permanent reinvention mindset. While I cultivated this mindset in sport, it can be applied to any endeavour.

In Western cultures, we consider outcomes as either good or bad. However, Eastern culture considers a balance of opposites. There is no good or bad, there is just cause and effect. Philosopher Alan Watts shared a wonderful story that encapsulates this phenomenon, called the Chinese Farmer. It goes as follows.

> *Once upon a time there was a Chinese farmer whose horse ran away. That evening, all of his neighbours came around to commiserate. They said, 'We are so sorry to hear your horse has run away. This is most unfortunate'. The farmer said, 'Maybe'.*
>
> *The next day the horse came back, bringing seven wild horses with it, and in the evening everybody came back and said, 'Oh, isn't that lucky. What a great turn of events. You now have eight horses!' The farmer again said, 'Maybe'.*
>
> *The following day his son tried to break one of the wild horses, and while riding it, he was thrown and broke his leg. The neighbours then said, 'Oh dear, that's too bad', and the farmer responded, 'Maybe'.*
>
> *The next day the conscription officers came around to conscript people into the army, and they rejected his son because he had a broken leg. Again, all the neighbours came around and said, 'Isn't that great!' Again, he said, 'Maybe'.*
>
> *'The whole process of nature is an integrated process of immense complexity, and it's really impossible to tell whether anything that happens in it is good or bad – because you never know what will be the consequence of the misfortune; or, you never know what will be the consequences of good fortune.'*
>
> —Alan Watts

The story reveals how we never know what will be the consequence of misfortune or of good fortune. Sometimes the things we really wish to happen could be the very things that ruin us. Sometimes the door that doesn't open is not our door.

To fulfil a vision, we must first exhaust all available avenues. We must expect obstacles as part of the process. Only when we have tried everything in our power and the path still remains blocked, is it time to try a different route.

The Tension of Opposites

Seventy-five percent of organisational transformation pro-grammes and eighty percent of new year's resolutions fail for a variety of reasons, but an understanding of the dynamic of oppo-sites is helpful when we encounter the blockers. We can expect pushback; if we don't, well then, maybe we are not pushing the boundaries quite far enough.

In the metamorphosis of the butterfly, there was tension between the emergent imaginal cells and the existing legacy cells of the caterpillar. When two counterforces meet they create energy, like the force created when polar opposites of a magnet repel each other. Physics tells us that, when two objects collide each exerts a force on the other, and these forces transfer energy between them. When you reframe resistance this way, you see that resistance is a natural part of any transformation.

According to Swiss physicist Heinrich Rohrer, 'Science means constantly walking a tightrope between blind faith and curiosity; between expertise and creativity; between bias and openness; between experience and epiphany; between ambition and passion; and between arrogance and conviction – in short, between an old today and a new tomorrow'.

Rohrer's quote encapsulates the tension of opposites. While he refers to science, this tension exists in every aspect of life: life and death, spring and summer, male and female, yin and yang. Rohrer's tightrope provides a useful metaphor. Imagine a tight-rope between two buildings. If the rope was slack, you would not want to walk across it. We need tension between the opposing ends of the tightrope to make it effective. When we embark on any change initiative, we walk such a tightrope.

Another useful mental model is that of a bow and arrow. When the string of the bow is taut, it provides enough tension to propel an arrow. Without that tension the arrow will not travel very far. By understanding this tension, we can harness the tense

Figure 8.2   Perpetual becoming

energy to thrust our vision into reality. In transformation we require a tension between old and new, certain and uncertain, order and chaos. Reinvention lives at the intersection of these tensions. All transformation requires this counterforce to drive effective change. This is the tension that exists within the infinity curve. There is an ongoing tension within the curve that serves as a dynamo that powers perpetual becoming.

Our challenges also exist on a continuum: the loftier the vision, the higher the hurdle, the greater the tension – but the greater the reward. Psychologist Carl Jung realised this when he said, 'The greater the contrast, the greater the potential. Great energy only comes from a correspondingly great tension of opposites'. Jung understood that the bigger our vision, the more obstacles we will need to overcome.

One of the obstacles to growth is that we become overly comfortable with the status quo and we cling to the familiar. Let's explore that next as we unpack crab curves.

Chapter Eight Takeaways

- As soon as we set a vision, we meet obstacles.
- The law of opposites gives us a powerful lens for the permanent reinvention mindset.

- When we understand there is a positive with every negative, when we inevitably encounter a negative, we know it is temporary and a positive experience is on the way.
- When you initiate change often people close to you will discourage you, they may see it as a reflection of themselves and won't want to let you go or grow. In other instances, they do not want to see you get hurt.
- It is difficult, but try not to hold it against them, they are playing the naysayer role that is common in any transformation process (with the caveat that if they are discouraging you on an ongoing basis, then you need to re-evaluate that relationship).
- In an organisation, this is akin to the blocker, the cell of the old DNA which blocks the emergent imaginal cell, also known as the corporate antibody.
- All crises, wars, pandemics, economic downturns are just negatives in a dynamic process, there is a positive on the way.
- When we realise the negative experience is a rite of passage on our journey toward success, we see the obstacles as milestones, not millstones.
- When two opposing forces collide they create energy – we can harness that energy to power a new reality.
- The loftier the vision, the higher the hurdles, but the greater the reward.

Questions

For the Individual

- How have you reacted when you encounter an obstacle?
- Do you see it as a sign that it is not meant to be or do you expect these challenges?
- Think back to any change you have initiated in your life, undoubtedly you have had support, but often have you been discouraged?

- If people close to you have discouraged you, do you hold it against them?
- Have you noticed that the loftier your goal, the higher the hurdles?
- Can you reframe obstacles as milestones now, rather than millstones?

For the organisation

- Have you anticipated the inevitable resistance that accompanies any change initiative?
- Have you considered where the status quo will resist?
- Have you looked in the mirror and challenged yourself? Are *you* resisting? Are you accepting organisational excuses?
- Are you more comfortable with managing the obstacles than pursuing the vision?
- Are you providing air cover for your changemakers, your imaginal cells? Remember, they are on the front line and they are the ones who encounter the resistance that creates the new power to propel your organisation into the future.
- Theirs is a lonely and challenging role; are you looking out for them?
- Have you identified who they are?
- Have you harnessed their energy?

9

Crab Curves

Figure 9.1 Leaving room to grow

'Death is nature's way of making things continually inter-esting. Death is the possibility of change. Every individual gets its allotted lifespan, its chance to try something new on the world. But time is called and the molecules which make

up leaf and limb, heart and eye are disassembled and redistributed to other tenants'.
—Peter Steinhart, *The Company of Wolves*

Have you ever seen an empty crab shell lying on the beach? Perhaps you mistook it for the remnants of a dead crab. It turns out the discarded shell does not signify the end of life, but marks the beginning of a new cycle.

Crabs are *invertebrates*, animals that don't have a backbone or spine. An *arthropod* is an *invertebrate* with an external skeleton called an exoskeleton. *Arthropods* include spiders, our friend the caterpillar and crustaceans such as lobsters and crabs. The exoskeleton of these animals is inelastic, so they eventually outgrow their shells. Just like the caterpillar, which moults its skin several times before the great metamorphosis into a butterfly, the crab sheds its shell as it evolves throughout its life.

The evolution of the crab provides a wonderful lens to consider how we outgrow our stations in life: our careers, our skill sets and our habits. I include organisations, because unless they provide people with scope to develop, they constrict growth.

Life's animating force compels us to evolve, but unlike the crab and the caterpillar, many of us ignore that inner calling to change. We hear the whispers in moments of silence: a walk in the wilderness, a moment in the shower, a vacant stare into the distance. We silence the voice with busyness, entertainment . . . anything but unearthing who we are destined to become. Instead of changing, we cling to the familiar, even though we are destined to evolve.

We Are One Hundred Trillion Cells

'How the past perishes is how the future becomes'.
—Alfred North Whitehead

The human body is composed of one hundred trillion (one trillion = one thousand times one billion) cells working in unison to create our bodies. Cells continually die and renew simultaneously. For example, three million red blood cells die every second. Our bodies contain different cells being replaced at varying rates. The average age of all cells in the human body is about seven years, some cells being more durable than others. If our body regenerates every seven years, what about us? What about our careers? What about our organisations?

Individual Shells

Just as the crab outgrows her shell, we all outgrow various stages of life. Somewhere along the way, we forget that. When we cling to a familiar shell it grates and irritates us. If we don't shed that shell, it imprisons our life force and our potential. For humans, an outgrown shell manifests in various ways, unique to each of us. Perhaps it is anger? Perhaps it is defensiveness? Perhaps you numb yourself to work but find meaning elsewhere?

Some of us reach the top of a career ladder and then spend our energy defending our status rather than continuing to evolve. Others find their roles boring and repetitive, but nonetheless choose to remain because it is secure and familiar or perhaps because it is what others expect of them. What lies ahead when you decide to go for it and discard the old shell? The evolution of the crab can enlighten us.

When a crab moults she hides for several days as her new shell hardens. During this time she is vulnerable to predation. Like the crab, when we discard our old shells we are also vulnerable. Our emergent self is susceptible to discouragement and doubt. There will be people who will dampen your spirit. The very people you expect to support you will do the opposite, 'Are you sure this is the right thing to do?' or 'Are you sure you want to give up that secure job with a global brand to work with a start-up no one has ever heard of?'

When we are in this emergent phase, it is vital to surround ourselves with people who support us. These are the people who see our bulging potential just waiting to emerge. These are the people who want to see us evolve.

Leadership Shells

In a 2018 interview, Amazon founder Jeff Bezos shared how his leadership style had changed over the years. He revealed that his leadership changed because it had to. He explained that a leader has to change in line with an evolving organisation. Bezos discarded the old shell of operations and embraced the new shell he calls teaching. In this teaching role, he focuses on culture, customer obsession and the future.

There are remarkable similarities between the evolution of the crab and Bezos' leadership style. Before her new shell hardens, the crab fills her tissues with water. This ensures her new shell is slightly larger than required so she has time to grow into it. This is akin to buying bigger-than-required clothes for a growing child, because they grow so quickly in those early years.

Bezos shared that he loves his job because he gets to work 'in the future'. He has constructed his job, so he is not 'pulled into the present'. This affords him the luxury of exploring edge behaviours, new trends and emerging technologies. In a way, he is creating a shell large enough for Amazon to grow into. Just as Bezos did this in his career, he orchestrated this mindset in his organisation. In February 2020, Bezos announced his retirement as CEO of the organisation he founded thirty years previously. In a move that surprised the business world, he said, "As Executive Chair (the new role he took up) I will stay engaged in important Amazon initiatives but also have the time and energy I need to focus on the Day 1 Fund, the Bezos Earth Fund, Blue Origin, The Washington Post, and my other passions." He added, "I've never had more energy, and this isn't about retiring. I'm super passionate about the impact I think these organizations can have."

The announcement signals Bezos' desire to grow into a bigger shell.

Business Model Shells

The crab metaphor works for business models too. Rather than exploring new growth opportunities or new 'shells', leaders get stuck managing today's shell as their main priority. They do so even when that shell is no longer (ahem) fit for purpose. This is the metaphorical rearranging of the deck chairs on the Titanic. The ship is still sinking, but damn, it will be in great shape when it does.

Even when organisations invest in new growth engines, they sometimes forget that the emergent stage is also the most vulnerable one, just like when a crab sheds its shell. Leaders must provide a safe haven for the fledgling business model and for those changemakers who are assigned to nurture it. Without such oversight, the organisational antibodies will attack the new idea and those who are working to bring it to life.

When new business models fail, leaders mistakenly believe that the idea must be flawed (and often they are), but they often overlook (and sometimes choose to overlook) a range of other factors. Sometimes a new business model fails because it never really had the resources, adequate time or protection it needed to survive. Other times, the people who report on an emergent business model have a vested interest in seeing it fail. It is the job of leadership to know the difference.

Amazon is an exemplar of evolving into larger and larger shells. Amazon started life selling books to consumers as a pipeline business. As it grew, the organisation shed that shell to become a platform business enabling other merchants to sell their goods. As Amazon built further capability and doubled down on customer obsession, it grew into an unstoppable organism. Today, it provides a platform for others, but continues to sell its own line of goods. Amazon has reinvented from a pipeline, to a platform, to a hybrid of both.

Despite phenomenal results, Bezos recognises that Amazon is not immune to decline: 'I predict one day Amazon will fail. Amazon will go bankrupt. If you look at large companies, their lifespans tend to be 30-plus years, not a hundred-plus years'. Bezos understands that everything has an allotted life span and everything must evolve. In theory, lobsters can live forever, they do not deteriorate with age. The problem they experience is a different one. Like crabs, lobsters shed their shell multiple times as they live their lives. However, they reach a point when they grow too big for their own shells. Shedding shells and growing new ones takes a lot of energy. Eventually, the amount of energy required to moult a shell and grow another is a step too far and the lobster succumbs to exhaustion, disease, predation or shell collapse.

As with lobsters, age can become a hindrance for organisations too. They find it increasingly difficult to reinvent on an ongoing basis. The goal of the permanent reinvention mindset is not to guarantee immortality but to avoid premature death, for that is the real tragedy.

Organisational Shells

Organisations are living entities, containing a mass of other living entities. Like the human body, they contain trillions of cells, all evolving at various rates. Just as there is an onus on individuals to reinvent, organisations must provide opportunities for people to grow.

One of the greatest inhibitors to personal growth is role speciality. When organisations hire people for their current expertise, they rarely provide opportunities for further expansion. When people remain stuck in their shell, with a set of stagnant accountabilities, their abilities atrophy. When the prospect for growth is limited, your best people will leave to pursue it elsewhere.

When organisations offer the possibility for development, both the organisation and the individual benefit. Employees stay with organisations longer when they experience growth, by enjoying various roles, travelling with the job or moving across departments. The organization benefits because the employee can share departmental knowledge across the organization. This is exactly what happens in Amazon. Ian Freed, who took huge risks in Amazon, used the knowledge gleaned for the Fire Phone experiment and used it in other innovations. This was a reason he joined Amazon and a reason he says that Amazon is very good at allowing people to move widely within the organisation so that they can learn, evolve and stay engaged. An extensive study into happiness and productivity found that workers are thirteen percent more productive when they are happy. As people grow, so does the organisation. As people develop new capabilities, so does the organisation. As people move across the organization, so does their knowledge.

On the flip side, just as the organisation has a responsibility to encourage people to move up, it also has a responsibility to encourage those who are stuck in their shells to move on.

Stuck in Our Shells?

During Jack Welch's time as CEO of General Electric, the company's stock value went up four thousand percent in twenty years. The company grew from twelve billion dollars to two hundred and eighty billion dollars as a result of, amongst other things, his decision to shift into emerging markets. Welch was ruthless when it came to bureaucracy and cut the number of employees by more than one hundred thousand in five years. Many people

Figure 9.2　Peak and prosper

criticised him, and even called him 'Jack the Ripper'. However, Welch said, 'You should be disciplined and get rid of the bottom ten percent of your employees each year. They may not think it, but you are doing them a favour because if they are not doing well with you, they need to move on'. While Welch was unpopular for this approach, but I agree with him. Sometimes, we get stuck in our familiar shells and a push is exactly what we need. It reminds me of the old story about the falcon who was stuck on its perch.

Once there was a king who received a gift of two magnificent falcons from Arabia. They were peregrine falcons, the most beautiful birds he had ever seen. He gave the precious birds to his head falconer to be trained.

Months passed and one day the head falconer informed the king that though one of the falcons was flying majestically, the other bird had not moved from its branch since the day it had arrived.

The king summoned healers and sorcerers from all over the land to tend to the falcon, but no one could make the bird fly. He presented the task to a member of his court, but the next day the king saw through the palace window that the bird had still not moved from its perch.

Having tried everything else, the king thought, 'Maybe I need someone more familiar with the countryside to understand the nature of this problem', so he told his court, 'go and get a farmer'.

In the morning, the king was thrilled to see the falcon soaring high above the palace gardens. He said to his court, 'Bring me the doer of this miracle'. The court quickly located the farmer, who came and stood before the king. The king asked him, 'How did you make the falcon fly?'

With his head bowed, the farmer said to the king, 'It was very easy, your highness. I simply cut the branch where the bird was sitting'.

Sometimes a crisis provides the burning platform we need to change our lives and grow into a new shell. When it happens, the crisis is all we can see, but in time we realise that it was exactly what we needed. We will explore this in Chapter Fifteen when we explore the story of Josephine Cochrane.

This happens in organisations too, sometimes a crisis unleashes latent potential. Sometimes we need others to cut the branch for us but it is always better to cut it ourselves. So why don't we do it more often? One of the biggest reasons is fear.

Chapter Nine Takeaways

- Crabs outgrow their shells and it is painful to stay in their shell once they outgrow them.
- Like crabs, we are made to evolve, we are made to move.
- When a crab removes its shell to grow a new one, it is vulnerable to predators.
- In a similar way, when we decide to evolve by changing career, ending a relationship or taking up a new hobby, people will criticise your decision.
- Remember, they are not attacking you, they think they are protecting you; in some cases your desire to change exposes their desire to stay still.
- Leaders must evolve throughout their careers. Jeff Bezos exemplifies this as he continually develops, discarding his old shell and embracing new ones.
- Amazon has shed and grown into new business models as it evolved: from a bookseller to a platform to a hybrid platform, amongst a plethora of other initiatives.
- Organisations must provide growth opportunities for their people, new shells for them to expand into.
- Organisations must also provide exit opportunities for those people who are stuck; helping them move on will help them find growth elsewhere.

Considerations

For the individual

- Have you outgrown your current shell?
- What are the symptoms of the ill-fitting shell?
- Is it impacting other areas of your life?
- Are you willing to cut your own branch or cling on in fear that someone will cut it for you?

For the organisation

- If you are a leader, are you delegating to your team, so that you do not outgrow your shell?
- Are you exploring the future to forge a new shell for your organisation?
- Are you simply rearranging the deck chairs on the Titanic?
- If you are overseeing a change programme, are your protecting the emergent business models?
- What about the changemakers, they need your help?
- Does your organisation offer growth opportunities?
- Do you encourage people to swim outside their swim lane of expertise? Can they move across the organisation?
- Each of your people will be at a different stage of their growth cycle; do you provide a one-size-fits-all growth programme or do you cater for their various learning styles?
- If people are stuck in their shells, do you have a strategy to cut their branches so they can find opportunities elsewhere?

10

Here Be Dragons

Figure 10.1   Here be dragons

'Nothing in life is to be feared. It is only to be understood'.
—Marie Curie

Centuries ago, mapmakers and cartographers didn't know the true shape of the seas and land. They worked outwards from the territories that were already explored. Back then, sailors went to sea with maps labelled with the Latin words *hic sun dracones* – here be dragons. Here be dragons meant we don't know much – if anything – about these uncharted lands.

In our increasingly uncertain world, we are continuously pushing the boundaries of what is known. Just as early explorers discovered the uncharted territories of the physical world, we are entering uncharted territories of the digital realm. While some of us find voyaging into the unknown exhilarating, others become paralysed by fear.

There is a reason I opened this chapter with the idea of the dragon. American writer, historian and mythologist Joseph Campbell extensively studied the presence of dragons in mythology. In the 1988 PBS series, The *Power of Myth*, Campbell explained how dragons guarded both gold and virgins, neither of which they could make use of. In a sense, the dragon squanders the gifts in its own possession. Campbell said, 'There's no vitality of experience . . . and you're captured in your own dragon cage'. This raises questions for all of us: Are we making use of our gifts or are we prisoners of our own dragons?

Dragons represent our fears, our ego, and anything else that holds us back (including our past, as we will explore in Chapter 16). Often, we are prisoners in the cave of our minds and fear is the dragon guarding the mouth of the cave. We must slay the dragon to get the gold. As thirteenth century Persian poet Rumi put it, 'Why do you stay in prison when the door is so wide open? Move outside the tangle of fear-thinking. The entrance door to the sanctuary is inside you'.

'There be dragons' all the way up your S curve towards your vision. The real tragedy is that some of us never embark on the journey because fear prevents us from beginning the odyssey in the first place.

The Ideal Road Not Taken

'When it comes time to die, let us not discover that we have never lived'.
—Henry David Thoreau

In a 2018 paper entitled, 'The Ideal Road Not Taken', psychologists at Cornell University revealed that people's biggest regrets come from the disparities between who they wanted to become and who they did become. The lead author of the study, Tom Gilovich, said 'When we evaluate our lives, we think about whether we're heading toward our ideal selves, becoming the person we'd like to be. Those are the regrets that are going to stick with you'. So why don't we act before it is too late?

When I run workshops, I ask participants, 'What keeps us from reinventing, from evolving, from pursuing our visions?' Participants range from C-suite executives to global leaders. I ask the same question in my lectures with master's students, who come from every corner of the globe. Despite the diversity of the groups, I invariably hear one of two answers: the dominant one is fear and the other one is shame. In a way, they are two sides of the same coin.

People are afraid that they will be wrong or they will feel ashamed if others think their ideas are stupid. Both reactions are influenced by fear. In life, fears manifest in our minds with questions like: What will my parents think? What will my friends think? What if I fail? These fear-based questions are common when we embark on any journey up a new curve. The undisruptable question we should be asking is: Would you rather live with the pain of failure or with the pain of regret? Fear is an inherent part of the S curve, it thrives in the embryonic stages of the journey, but it loses its power as you progress.

In an evolutionary sense, fear of real danger is useful for survival. It keeps us safe and ensures we avoid dangerous situations. However, fear of a future outcome is limiting. Too much fear can cause psychological discomfort, mental health problems and lifelong regrets.

The permanent reinvention mindset requires us to reframe fear as growing pains. What if the feeling of fear was not a signal to stop but rather an indication that we were on the verge of new growth?

Reframing Fear

In an interview with David Bowie, a reporter asked what advice he would offer for aspiring artists. Bowie replied: 'If you feel safe in the area you're working in, you're not working in the right area. Always go a little further into the water than you feel you're capable of being in. Go a little out of your depth, and when you don't feel that your feet are quite touching the bottom, you're just about in the right place to do something exciting'.

Recently, my sons and I explored an Irish woodland. I jumped across a small stream and continued, but my son had stopped on the other side. He stared at the drop below and said was afraid to jump. I asked him to tell me how he physically felt. He described butterflies in his stomach and his heart beating really fast. I asked him to think about how he felt when he was excited about something, like Christmas morning. Once again, he described butterflies in his stomach and how his heart beats really fast. I said nothing further and just smiled.

A smile appeared on his face. He realised they were both the same physical feelings. I explained that feelings are the language of the body and thoughts are the language of the mind. Sometimes, we have the same feelings for different experiences in life, but it is how we frame those feelings that makes the difference. I also made sure that he understood that fear is also a mental construct to ensure we are safe. So, in this case his mind didn't want him to get hurt, so it made that small leap feel like a bigger ordeal than it really was. With a little guidance, he reframed this small fear as a growth opportunity. (I hope he did anyway, or else I just confused the poor guy . . . again.) Once we learn to reframe fear, we can become increasingly accustomed to it.

The Dose Makes the Poison – What Doesn't Kill You Makes You Stronger

'The dose makes the poison' is a term attributed to Swiss physicist Paracelsus. He claimed that 'poisons' were not necessarily negative because it was the dose that determined if a substance was poisonous or not.

My younger son has a nut allergy, and to increase his tolerance we follow a 'nut exposure programme'. Every day we feed him increasing amounts of various nuts over set periods of time. The aim is to boost his tolerance by increasing the exposure levels. It is a useful way to think about fear also.

Hormesis is a process whereby a beneficial effect (improved health, stress tolerance, growth or longevity) results from exposure to low doses of a toxin. Regarding my son's nut exposure therapy, hormesis is the introduction of low doses of nuts (toxin) over time. Initially he may feel negative effects, but over time he will adapt to the stressor. In time, he will become increasingly resilient to that toxin.

Hormesis has been studied extensively with aging. Researchers found that the introduction of stressors – intermittent fasting, exercise and cold shower therapy, for example – produces anti-ageing effects. For example, when an optional cold shower activates mild fight or flight responses, it increases our tolerance for the cold and can guard us from catching a cold. Just as we can build up our tolerance for poisons, we can increase our tolerance for fear.

As with hormesis, instead of reaching a certain point and recoiling back toward safety, we venture just far enough to get used to a new tolerance level. As Bowie said, we just let our feet touch the bottom and then we push the boundaries once we become comfortable. In time, we will become used to our new fear tolerance level and continue to build on this. We venture into unchartered lands and slay the dragons on our own terms.

This is the spirit of the infinity curve. There is no destination. Every time we become comfortable, yes we enjoy the crest of the wave, but we do not sit still, we do not stagnate, we do not atrophy. We add a little more discomfort until we become comfortable with it once again. But what happens when we are not in charge of the challenges, when we encounter a negative and unexpected experience? We can reframe those situations also.

Post-Traumatic Growth

'The mind, once stretched by a new idea, never returns to its original dimensions'.

—Ralph Waldo Emerson

Post-traumatic growth (PTG) refers to the positive psychological change we experience when we overcome painful challenges. Studies show a positive correlation between stressful life

Figure 10.2   Get comfortable being uncomfortable

events and personal growth. In a study called 'The Assessment and Prediction of Stress-Related Growth', participants described the aftermath of their stressful events as: 'I rethought how I want to live my life'; 'I learned to be open to new information and ideas'; 'I learned that I want to have some impact on the world'. Slaying the dragon does not always turn out the way we had hoped. The point is that we venture out of the cave, we don't remain a prisoner and spend our life wondering what might have happened.

It often takes a crisis to push us beyond our boundaries as we will see with Josephine Cochrane in Chapter Fifteen, but why wait for a crisis? The permanent reinvention mindset encourages us to stage crises within our control, before we encounter those beyond our control. Reframing fear builds up our resilience to deal with unexpected events and minimises the impact of such events on our lives and in our organisations. In the next chapter we will explore how Fujifilm prepared for a crisis years before it arrived by building capability and using their existing capabilities in novel ways.

Chapter Ten Takeaways

- Mapmakers used to mark unknown territories with the words 'Here Be Dragons'.
- Dragons represent the waste of talent or gifts that we have in our possession.
- Many of us do this with our capabilities: we hoard them and remain prisoners to our fears.
- By reframing fears as growing pains we become increasingly tolerant of fear.
- In organisations, many senior executives are paralysed by the fear of mistakes.
- Fear is a mental construct to keep us safe; just as we form fears, we can dissolve them over time.

Considerations

For the individual

- How can you introduce a bit of fear into your life? Start small. Perhaps it is trying a new food or new hobby.
- Perhaps you fear what people will think if you wear a new piece of clothing or cut your hair a certain way.
- Next, can you try public speaking? Start a blog or a podcast? Share some paintings?
- Eventually, you might start a side business, but it doesn't even need to be a big leap.
- If you are a parent, how do you introduce a bit of discomfort for your children?
- Sitting comfortably does not prepare them for the real world, a little discomfort helps them to evolve.
- What about in work, do you fear speaking up? Is that your fear or does the organisation discourage it?

For the organisations

- Like sailors embarking on odysseys into uncharted land, this age of VUCA is a mental odyssey into the unknown.
- Fear is natural as you push yourself out of your comfort zone.
- Every jump to a new curve should involve some discomfort. If you stop feeling fear, ask yourself, are you pushing yourself far enough?
- If you are resting comfortably on the peak of your S curve, is it the fear of failure that is keeping you there?
- What about your people, do you have a psychologically safe workplace where people do not fear speaking up or suggesting new ideas?

PART 3

Undisruptable in Action

11

The Immortal Jellyfish: Fujifilm

'Every act of creation is first an act of destruction'.
—Pablo Picasso

The only animal we know that is capable of reverting back to a younger version of itself is called *Turritopsis Dohrnii* or 'the immortal jellyfish'. The immortal jellyfish follows the normal life cycle of a jellyfish all the way until it reaches maturity. As you can see in Figure 11.1, it maps nicely to the S curve phases.

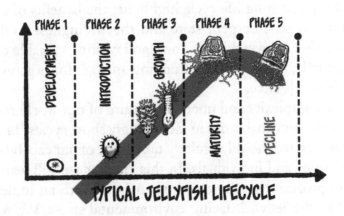

Figure 11.1   Typical jellyfish life cycle

Figure 11.2   Immortal jellyfish life cycle

When faced with death, it willingly reverts to a sexually immature stage and starts its life cycle all over again. In doing so, it discards the mature parts of its body – its limbs and tentacles and plunges back to the ocean floor to become a baby polyp once again.

The immortal jellyfish initiates this cycle when faced with environmental stress, such as starvation or injury. In the laboratory, researchers have observed how adult *Turritopsis* regularly undergo this change, renewing themselves frequently. Therefore, if they can avoid predation and disease, theoretically they can live forever.

This fascinating life cycle highlights the benefits of a regular return to an emergent state and the willingness to discard elements that are weighing it down and wasting valuable energy. Conceptually, this provides a stunning analogy for organisations and individuals alike.

The complexity and uncertain nature of our world requires us to renew our capabilities in increasingly short cycles. This new reality means we should regularly take stock of our capabilities as organisations and individuals. In this chapter we will learn how Fujifilm proactively reinvented when faced with an impending crisis, like the jellyfish facing environmental stress. We will see how Amazon willingly unbundled capabilities to create the AWS (Amazon Web Services) growth engine. Finally, we will explore what this means for us and our careers in the future.

Unbundling Capabilities

At face value, we may think we only have one business model, one product or one role. But each of these outputs consists of multiple interlocking inputs. When we break them into their constituent parts, we can reconfigure them to create new and interesting combinations. What's more, we can identify and then add missing ingredients that could take us in entirely different directions.

Think of a business model, organisation or career as interlocking pieces of LEGO. While we can combine them to form various structures, only six rectangular 4x2 LEGO bricks offer a massive 915,103,765 combinations. Before you figure out what you are going to build you need to take stock of three things: your LEGO pieces, your imagination, and your willingness to experiment. When we embrace this mindset, it can deliver spectacular results, as Fujifilm discovered over the last three decades.

Immortal Fujifilm

'In an often unpredictable business world, a peak always conceals a treacherous valley'.

—Shigetaka Komori (Former CEO, Fujifilm)

In the year 2000, photographic products delivered sixty percent of Fujifilm's sales and seventy percent of its profit. Within a decade, digital cameras destroyed that business. In 2012, Fujifilm's old sparring partner, Kodak, filed for bankruptcy. Yet Fujifilm continues to go from strength to strength. How did Fujifilm succeed where so many others failed and what does it have to do with the immortal jellyfish?

Fujifilm appointed Shigetaka Komori as CEO at their most vulnerable point in history. After multiple rounds of cost-cutting, plant closures and redundancies, Komori knew he could not cost-cut the company into the future. Instead, Fujifilm chose an undisruptable route.

In a stellar display of reinvention, Fujifilm unbundled their capabilities, which included patents in chemical compounds and nanotechnology. Next, they systematically sought to apply previously built capabilities in novel ways. As a result of these efforts, today the organisation enjoys successful interests in healthcare, life sciences, pharmaceuticals, regenerative medicine, and even a Covid-19 vaccine. While they still maintain a small footprint in business areas related to their legacy products – such as digital cameras, instant photo systems and digital recording equipment – that only accounts for minor revenues. To demonstrate how they unbundled capability, let's examine how they stumbled upon their hit category: beauty.

> 'We put a very strong anti-oxidation ingredient into our photographic products in order to stop the colour from fading as time goes by, and we decided to do this for our skincare products too'.
> —Shigetaka Komori (Former CEO, Fujifilm)

On the surface beauty products appear to be a an entirely unrelated business to photography. However (ahem), looks can be deceiving. Fujifilm discovered that some key ingredients of film could be used to enter the field of beauty. The four basic film-related technologies that Fujifilm used to develop beauty products were collagen research, light analysis and control, antioxidation, and original nanotechnology. After years creating film products, entire departments suddenly found themselves developing beauty products. In 2007, Fujifilm boldly launched a high-end skincare range called ASTALIFT. With a subtle hat-tip to their origins, ASTALIFT aims to deliver 'Photogenic Beauty' to its customer. Long before Kodak filed for bankruptcy in 2012, Fujifilm was enjoying diversified annual revenues of over $20 billion with only a minor contribution coming from photographic products. When we think of their bold S curve jump, ASTALIFT involved a brave step backwards that resulted in an incredible stride forwards. In 2020, Fujifilm reported revenues of $22.1 billion, with Global healthcare including cosmetics contributung twenty-two percent or \$4.9 billion to that sum. Fujifilm sees cosmetics as a growing part of their offering and continues to invest in a diversified future.

We can learn a lot from Fujifilm's success. By taking stock of the ingredients we have at our disposal, we can identify interesting combinations. When this approach is coupled with an openness to pursue opportunities and accept failure, it can yield remarkable results. However, there is one important element of the Fujifilm success story that is essential, but often overlooked.

Remember the undisruptable mantra from Chapter Three, 'build capability before we need it'? Remember how we must develop new capabilities while we are on the way up the curve, not when we encounter decline? The Spartan warrior mantra, repopularised by American General Norman Schwarzkopf, encapsulates it well: 'The more you sweat in peace, the less you bleed in war'. Fujifilm did all of these things, building capability before it encountered a crisis and investing heavily in research and development while it had revenues to do so. However, it is important to recognise that the CEO at the time, Shigetaka Komori didn't initiate the transformation process, although he still deserves huge credit. The transformation had started long before he received the baton.

THE MORE YOU SWEAT IN PEACE, THE LESS YOU BLEED IN WAR

SCHWARZKOPF

Figure 11.3 Sweat in peace

Komori's predecessor was Minoru Ohnishi. Ohnishi became CEO in 1980, and it was Ohnishi who paved the way for the success Fujifilm enjoyed decades later. Next, let's explore why Ohnishi built new capabilities long before they were required.

During the 1970s the photography business was rocked to its core when the price of silver jumped tenfold, from five dollars to fifty dollars per ounce. Silver was an essential ingredient in photo-processing and manufacturers like Kodak and Fujifilm feared their businesses were in jeopardy. When the price plummeted again in 1980, Kodak and the other photographic businesses settled back to business as usual. Because they enjoyed success, they soon overlooked the crisis as a blip. This was not how Fujifilm's new CEO, Ohnishi, viewed the event.

Ohnishi prepared the organisation for a radical shift in the photography business. Once Sony introduced its digital camera in 1984, he was utterly convinced Fujifilm had no choice but to reinvent. With total conviction, Fujifilm set to work building diverse digital capabilities. To show the extent of their commitment to the future, consider that by 2003, Fujifilm had nearly five thousand mini digital processing labs in chain stores throughout the U.S. while Kodak had fewer than one hundred.

As Ohnishi built Fujifilm's capabilities before the imminent crisis, he experienced the inevitable resistance that accompanies such a large-scale transformation. As Jack Welch did in General Electric, Ohnishi led the business process transformation in tandem with Fujifilm's diversification efforts. By the time Ohnishi handed the baton to Komori, the flywheel was well and truly in motion and Komori built on that momentum.

Fujifilm's success highlights so many traits of the permanent reinvention mindset. They embraced kintsugi thinking, understanding that not all their bets would pay off. They overcame obstacles and fear. Komori said, 'You have to be brave to carry out changes. You shouldn't be scared by problems, and you shouldn't fear danger'. Fujifilm was proactive in building capability long before it was needed, a move that catapulted them ahead of their competitors. What is especially salient about the Fujifilm story is how they unbundled and rebundled their capabilities to spectacular effect, adding missing elements through mergers, acquisitions, learning new skills and unlearning old ones.

Before we explore the lessons for our careers, let's see how like Fujifilm, Amazon unbundled capabilities to grow the business, rather than protect it from an imminent storm. Amazon used existing capabilities to unearth what became their biggest growth engine: Amazon Web Services.

The Multi-Billion Dollar Meeting

In 2003, a group of senior Amazon executives gathered in the home of Jeff Bezos. One of the agenda items of their business retreat was to identify the company's existing competencies. This meeting would change the direction of the company and fuel it to become the trillion-dollar organisation we know today.

Back then, Bezos' chief of staff was Andy Jassy. Jassy was announced CEO of Amazon in February 2021. Jassy has been with Amazon since 1997 and was CEO of Amazon Web Services (AWS) before becoming Amazon CEO. To this day, he pinpoints that meeting as a pivotal moment that radically changed the business. The senior team recognised they had become highly competent at running infrastructure services like storage, database and scalable data centres. Amazon had developed these capabilities because of an internal need, to speed up deployment of new applications and services at the lowest possible cost. In the meeting, the senior team reframed these other skills in an entirely different way.

Science fiction novelist Isaac Asimov reportedly once said, 'The most exciting phrase to hear in science, the one that heralds new discoveries, is not "Eureka!" but "That's funny"'. That is exactly how the Amazon team reacted. While that reaction may seem innocuous, it takes a certain mindset to identify and then pursue opportunities like this. You must be open to possibilities, willing to accept failure and be insatiably curious. With these skills in abundance, slowly and surely Amazon began putting some shape on a business that would provide infrastructure services to developers.

Today that business, AWS, is a leading provider of cloud computing in the company of Microsoft Azure and Google Cloud. AWS has experienced unforeseen growth year on year, albeit slightly impacted in Q2 2020 due to the Covid-19 pandemic. Nevertheless, in that quarter AWS revenue hit $10.8 billion, which was up twenty-nine percent year on year. '$43 billion annualized run rate business, up nearly $10 billion in run rate in the last 12 months', according to Amazon CFO Brian Olsavsky. Not bad for an idea that sprouted from a core capabilities meeting less than two decades ago.

A core capability meeting is a common practice for undisruptable organisations (and individuals). A McKinsey taskforce researched the most common traits of the world's best growth companies. The forty subject companies demonstrated revenue increases of twenty-five percent per year. What was one of their success characteristics? To 'assemble a platform of capabilities'. Undisruptable organisations take stock of broader capabilities, including growth-enabling skills and capabilities, but also privileged assets and special relationships as key building blocks in undisruptability. Growth companies never rest on the laurels of success, and if they are missing skill sets they develop them internally or through partnership and acquisition.

Top of Your Game?

We have established that unbundling core competencies is a valuable exercise for organisations. The same principle can be applied to our roles. With the onset of artificial intelligence and automation, it is not roles that will be replaced, but various tasks within those roles. Many roles that were considered safe in the past will disappear in the future. The more rote and repetitive the tasks within a role, the quicker an algorithm will learn and

Figure 11.4   Develop capability

replace those roles. Developing diverse competencies, before the need to develop them becomes critical, offers competitive advantage.

While organisations should encourage role diversification, moving employees regularly throughout the organisations so that they acquire various skill sets, the ultimate responsibility lies with the individual. This goes for all of us, from CEO to intern. There is nobody in the organisation lying awake at night wondering, 'I wonder if Aidan is learning enough in his role?' We are responsible for developing our own capability.

For those of us who believe we are safe in well-established and secure roles, this may seem counterintuitive. Why develop capabilities and acquire diverse knowledge when we are doing so well? 'If I'm top of my game, why would I bother learning about trends that are irrelevant to my current focus?' That is the danger zone, that is 'top of the S curve thinking', and that's where we have blind spots. The more proactive we are about building capabilities, the more adaptive we will be when we need those skills. So, how do we diversify our capabilities to become undisruptable? We can take some lessons from business model diversification.

A Portfolio of Capabilities

While it is wise to diversify business interests, it is even better when you also diversify business models. This is an important distinction: a business model is not product. A product can have multiple business models. For example, Nestlé is the parent company of both Nespresso and Nescafé. Nespresso sells coffee pods direct to consumers and branded boutique stores via a subscription model. Meanwhile, Nescafé sells via the traditional method of B2B to suppliers and partners. This means Nestlé enjoys a portfolio of business models, not just a portfolio of brands. In a world of disruption, the difference is crucial, because if a business model is disrupted, it does not drag the entire organisation down with it. A portfolio of business models means, if one business model declines the others can keep delivering.

Now hold that thought and relate it to role diversification, where the same principle applies. When we only have one string to our professional bow, we are at risk of career disruption. When our roles are made of repeatable tasks, we are susceptible to automation. This means a portfolio of capabilities provides some comfort in turbulent times.

Take, for example, digital capabilities. Many of us have heard how important these skills are, yet very few of us were proactive about developing them. When the turbulent period caused by Covid-19 took us by surprise, many of us found ourselves unprepared. This is what legendary investor Warren Buffet meant when he quipped, 'Only when the tide goes out do you discover who's been swimming naked'. Some of us were (and still might be) winging it on outdated capabilities and some of us were getting by on defunct business models. My message is don't wait for the storm to hit, get ahead of it. Increasingly, we will see companies hire for learnability and train for skill.

'The illiterate of the 21st century will not be those who cannot read and write, but those who cannot learn, unlearn, and relearn'.

—Alvin Toffler

This may seem like unnecessary work and you may believe your role is secure, but remember the deceptive nature of exponential change. Remember the IBM skills gap study: '120 million workers in the world's twelve largest economies will need to upskill in the next three years because of artificial intelligence'. The good news is that it is never too late to build new capabilities and it has never been easier, with so many inexpensive ways to do so at our disposal.

Artificial intelligence will creatively destruct by destroying old roles and creating new ones. Therefore, we have to be like the immortal jellyfish and willingly descend to the beginning of the S curve, discarding old skills that are no longer relevant and building new ones that will be. The question to ask yourself is, do you want to be a Kodak or do you want to be a Fujifilm?

Before we look at how Arnold Schwarzenegger and Walt Disney built portfolios of capabilities and how Josephine Cochrane was pushed by a crisis to conquer fear, let's see how Nokia and BlackBerry stopped evolving once they reached their peak and as a result, they were defeated by victory.

Chapter Eleven Takeaways

- The immortal jellyfish is capable of reverting to a younger state at will and does so when it senses an impending threat by plunging to the bottom of the ocean to begin a new life cycle.
- This provides a stunning analogy for organisational and personal development.
- In a VUCA age, we don't have time to wait for a crisis to develop new capabilities, we need to do so before it becomes necessary.
- Fujifilm did this to great effect, by first developing their digital capabilities while their peers sat back and on the peak of success.

- Fujifilm went a step further and unbundled and rebundled their capabilities in novel ways.
- This process gave rise to their diverse revenue stream in beauty, healthcare and elsewhere.
- Amazon took stock of their capabilities over two decades ago to plant the seeds for what became Amazon Web Services, a wildly successful part of the Amazon machine.
- While organisations have a responsibility to avoid role specialisation and encourage employees to diversify their skills, the ultimate responsibility for upskilling and learning is ours.
- A good way to think of competencies is as business models: the more diverse your business models, the less likely you are to experience disruption.
- If one business model declines, you have others that will carry you through a crisis.
- This is no different for skill sets, where artificial intelligence will replace tasks and not roles: therefore, the more diverse the tasks within your role, the more secure your role.

Considerations

For the individual

- Are your capabilities applicable in a number of industries or just one?
- If it is just one industry, where is that industry on its S curve?
- Have you ever assessed your capabilities?
- Perhaps you never had to, but it can turn your life in an entirely new and exciting direction.
- To assess your capabilities try this exercise:

Step 1: Take a pack of Post-it notes.
Step 2: Unbundle the tasks, skills, relationships, competencies, habits, and disciplines that make up your role.

Step 3: Add some hobbies and desired skills to the Post-its.

Step 4: Write down some possible roles or industries that interest you.

Step 5: Rebundle your capabilities, by reconfiguring the Post-it notes and see what interesting combinations you can come up with.

Step 6: Cross-reference your favourite combinations with some existing roles.

Step 7: If there are gaps, explore how you can fill them through learning, asking for new projects within your organisation or seeking internships while you are a student.

For the organisation

- Have you unbundled your organisations capabilities?
- Have you considered the skill sets and capabilities required for your industry in the future?
- Are you aware of the most desirable skills in this age of VUCA?
- Have you assigned any budget to upskilling your people?
- To assess your capabilities try this exercise as an executive team. (Remember permanent reinvention isn't only a matter of developing new capabilities, it is also about rewiring existing capabilities to create new combinations.)

Step 1: Take a pack of Post-it notes

Step 2: Unbundle the tasks, skills, relationships, partners, patents, activities, segments, channels, competencies, habits, budgets, disciplines that make up your organisation. (I recommend the timeless use of Alex Osterwalder's 'Business Model Generation'.)

Step 3: Write down some possible industries or products that you could enter with low-cost experiments.

Step 5: Reconfigure the Post-it notes and see what interesting combinations you can come up with.

Step 6: Cross-reference your top five combinations with some adjacent business opportunities.

Step 7: Come up with two step-change opportunities, disruptive opportunities, wild cards.

Step 8: If there are gaps, how can you fill them?

Step 9: Do you have resources in-house that could be tweaked or retrained?

Step 10: Do this regularly.

12

Defeated by Victory: Nokia

*'The arrogance of success is to think that what you did yester-
day will be sufficient for tomorrow'.*
                                        —William Pollard

In November 2007, Forbes ran a cover story entitled, 'One
billion customers, can anyone catch the cell phone king?'. That
year the S&P stock index was up only five percent but Nokia's
stock surged one hundred and fifty-five percent with a peak stock
price of around forty dollars per share. Two years later, the share
price had dropped below ten dollars. Within eight years, the
share price plummeted below five dollars and Nokia offloaded
its once-dominant smartphone business to Microsoft.

What went wrong, and what can we learn from this tragic
case of disruption? We will dissect the affair through the lens of S
curves, but before we do, let's briefly explore how Nokia climbed
to the top in the first place.

Nokia's history dates back to 1865, when it began life as a
pulp mill in Finland. The company inherited the name of the
neighbouring town of Nokia and the nearby river Nokianvirta.
After World War I, Nokia was on the verge of bankruptcy when
it was acquired by the Finnish Rubber Works. Then, in 1932,

the Finnish Rubber Works acquired the Finnish Cable Works. In 1967, The Nokia Corporation was formed by merging these three companies.

Throughout its diverse history, the Nokia Corporation excelled in a variety of sectors, from toilet paper to textiles, rubber boots to electronic equipment and cabling. This diversification eventually culminated in the company's hit product when it launched the mobile phone.

When you plot some of Nokia's products on a series of S Curves it looks as follows. (See Figure 12.1 below).

Nokia progressed slowly up the mountain through a varied and diversified portfolio. The organisation had overcome significant setbacks, such as world wars and countless other disruptions, along the way. They had displayed remarkable resilience to achieve well-earned market dominance. So, what happened when Nokia shifted to a primary focus on telecommunications in the 1990s? Success, hubris and a toxic culture played a part, but most of all Nokia grew fearful of deviation away from their successful product and began defending success. Nokia was on top of the mobile telephone S curve, an industry they had moulded. They became complacent and were eventually defeated by their victory with the Nokia mobile handset. They

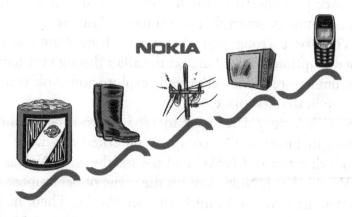

Figure 12.1   Nokia curves

Figure 12.2   Nokia stock 2007–2020 'long-kiss-goodnight'

also clutched tightly to legacy distribution and business models, selling handsets through telecom carriers while the industry evolved around them. Figure 12.2 above shows their magnificent rise and momentous fall.

Their peak was in November 2007, just before Forbes ran that cover story 'One billion customers, can anyone catch the cell phone king?'. Just look at what happened subsequently. I call this a 'long-kiss-goodnight' curve (Figure 12.2 above), where the peak not only plummets sharply, but is stretched out over years of painful decline as the company teeters along like the slower and slower beeps on a heart rate monitor. This is death by a thousand cuts. It is a slow painful decline as the company optimises through rounds of cost-cutting, redundancies and asset sales, as their iceberg slowly melts. (There are still some successful parts of Nokia today and some green shoots of rebirth.)

In a 2016 letter to shareholders, Jeff Bezos declared that Amazon must stay in 'Day One'. He said, 'Staying in day one requires you to experiment patiently, accept failures, plant seeds, protect saplings'. Day one is the exciting, curious, energetic stage we experience when we start something new. In the S curve model it is the early phases, but as Bezos recognises, we need to maintain that mindset. Bezos goes on to describe the characteristics of 'Day Two' companies, that included words like, 'irrelevance, stasis, excruciating, painful decline and eventually death'. This was where Nokia found themselves; despite their unprecedented success, they were deeply entrenched in day two.

In an infamous interview, an interviewer quizzed former CEO of Nokia Stephen Elop about their new product lines. The interviewer revealed that he had an iPhone, to which Elop responded, 'How embarrassing!' With that, he took the iPhone from the interviewer and flung it onto the studio floor. A few years later, it was the Nokia share price that was on the floor.

The lesson here is not so much that Nokia fell from the peak of the mountain, but that the mountain they ruled had so quickly become a molehill. The tectonic plates of disruption recalibrated the landscape and Nokia was simply not prepared for the dramatic change, despite the numerous signals they chose to ignore. Some of these signals will surprise you; let's explore them next.

Figure 12.3   Nokia king of the mountain

'It was very early days, and no one really knew anything about the touch screen's potential. And it was an expensive device to produce, so there was more risk involved for Nokia. So management did the usual. They killed it'.

—Ari Hakkarainen (Nokia employee who sought
Nokia executive support for a touchscreen device)

The Nokia story, like so many other victims of disruption, is one of potential lost. The mobile king had the talent, the money, the existing capabilities, connections and customers and even the foresight to make the transition. Despite all this, one of the most frustrating elements of the Nokia story is that senior engineers presented a touch screen mobile phone to senior management in 2004, years before the iPhone appeared in 2007. I interviewed Columbia Professor Rita McGrath, who worked as a consultant with Nokia at the time. Rita said she not only saw this device, but held it in her hands. To add insult to injury, Nokia's forward-thinking engineers had even presented the idea of a virtual store, where users could download these things called apps or applications and what's more that would provide a new revenue stream. So why did Nokia miss it?

It is a story reminiscent of Henry Ford's motorcar and the horse in Chapter Three. Like the first motorcars, the iPhone initially was a poor performer in terms of call quality, battery life, and network usage compared with Nokia and BlackBerry. But Moore's law – exponential improvement in technology and shifting customer needs – soon reconfigured the marketplace and Nokia's mountain became a molehill. When combined with their 'day two behaviours', including outdated leadership, slow decision making and defunct business models with a generous helping of hubris, the end was near for Nokia.

When Nokia and its peers, such as BlackBerry, eventually included iPhone-like features in their devices they struggled. They became prisoners of their past: past business and mental models, past designs and past success. Nokia was creating devices that included elements of their old design, while Apple and newcomers such as Samsung were designing devices for a new paradigm.

Figure 12.4   Nokia king of the molehill

Nokia tried to win by defending hard-fought victories. Physiologically, when we are defensive, our minds become closed to new information even when it is important to our survival. We might even dismiss our very own development team who present to us the perfect product at the right time. Nokia had stopped evolving and started dying, but alas, they were far from alone.

BlackBerry Blues – The Arrogance of Success

> 'It's kind of one more entrant into an already very busy space with lots of choice for consumers . . . But in terms of a sort of a sea-change for Black-Berry, I would think that's overstating it'.
> —Jim Balsillie on the iPhone in February 2007

In 2008, Research in Motion, the creators of the BlackBerry phone, enjoyed 44.5% of the mobile phone market. The iPhone had just launched and Google's Android operating system was in its infancy. BlackBerry revenues had doubled year on year to $6 billion. Over the next three years, BlackBerry saw revenues triple, reaching a peak of almost $20 billion. You can see where this is going.

Today, like Nokia, BlackBerry survives as a shadow of its former self, with revenues hovering around $1 billion. The 'long kiss goodnight curve' (Figure 12.5) looks similar to the Nokia graph (Figure 12.2 above), with a slow gradual climb to the top of the mountain followed by a dramatic fall from the peak.

One of the many lessons we can learn from the rise and fall of BlackBerry is, as with Nokia: once you achieve success, your victory can defeat you. This is especially the case if your success is accompanied by hubris.

The co-CEO of BlackBerry during those glory years was Jim Balsillie. In an interview with Balsillie in 2008, an interviewer suggested that the recently launched iPhone was not the threat that some commentators believed it would be. He went on to ask Balsillie what RIM would do if they needed to diversify beyond the BlackBerry. Balsillie's response said it all: he said rather than diversify they would 'preferably die'. He said, 'We

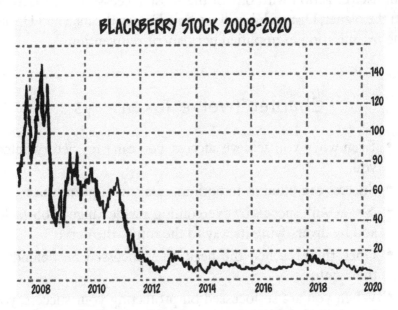

Figure 12.5   BlackBerry long kiss goodnight curve 2008–2020

are a very poorly diversified portfolio. It either goes to the moon or it crashes to the earth'. And crash to the earth it certainly did.

History is littered with organisations (and individuals) that became blinkered by their success. The success trap can cause us to lose the hunger that helped us achieve our vision in the first place. Once we reach our vision or stumble upon success, we mistakenly believe the job is done. To stay on the infinity curve, we must stay hungry, keep learning and continually evolve. We must learn to let go of business models and mental models that served us in the past, to make way for new ones that will fuel us in the future.

The failure to diversify business models and capabilities was a fatal flaw for both Nokia and BlackBerry. Nokia's story shows that, even when you get to the top of mountain thanks to a diverse portfolio, once you stop evolving you start declining. BlackBerry gloated about their lack of product diversification, and it was that same lack of diversity that hastened their demise several years later.

In the next chapter, we will see the permanent reinvention mindset in action with one of the most successful organisations on the planet, Disney. We will see how Disney the man and Disney the organisation exemplified permanent reinvention.

Chapter Twelve Takeaways

- Even when you achieve success, you can't let victory defeat you.
- Success can blind us to both threats and opportunities.
- Nokia built success by overcoming a wide range of obstacles and by diversifying its way to the top of the curve.
- Once they reached the peak, they focussed on defending their status.
- When you are so focussed on protecting your success, you become blind to threats and opportunities.

- Jeff Bezos said Amazon needs to stay in day one; day one entails all the characteristics we need on the journey up an S curve: vision, hunger, humility and a beginner's mind.
- Day two is characterised by stasis, irrelevance and death, the characteristics of the top of an S curve. These are lessons both Nokia and BlackBerry, and so many others, have learned the hard way.

Considerations

For the individual

- How have you behaved when you reached a peak?
- Did you become complacent?
- When someone suggested new ways of doing things that were contrary to your existing beliefs, how did you react?
- Did you listen or did you selectively listen for what was wrong with their suggestion?
- You probably know someone who behaves like this, someone who 'already knows' what you are trying to share with them.
- How does that make you feel?

For the organisation

- Is your strategy defensive of offensive?
- When you achieve success, do you batten down the hatches and defend it?
- Think back to how you got to where you are: are you still in day one?
- Are you showing signs of day two?
- If you are successful, are you humble about your success?
- Put yourself in the shoes of Nokia's leadership: an engineer presents a new way of doing things; how do you react?

13

Di'S'ney Curves

'A person should set his goals as early as he can and devote all his energy and talent to getting there. With enough effort, he may achieve it. Or he may find something that is even more rewarding. But in the end, no matter what the outcome, he will know he has been alive'.

—Walt Disney

Walt Disney came from humble beginnings to achieve phenomenal success. He was the first to add sound and colour to animation, to create a feature-length animated movie, to reinvent the theme park and so much more. He followed the path of reinvention, driven by a vision, managing contrasts, facing fear, building capabilities and reinventing himself along the way.

To learn from his journey, we will plot his progress onto a series of S curves. We will see how not every leap yielded financial success. Sometimes the success was the skills he and his teams developed in the attempt, or as we now call it: return on capability. Whether he was aware of it or not, those skills fuelled his future endeavours.

Building Capability

The year was 1910 and ten-year-old Walt Disney lived in Kansas City. He began each day at 3:15 a.m. as a paperboy. His family was poor, so his paper round contributed towards the household bills. His passions included drawing, comic books, amusement parks, acting, and movies. To fuel these passions, he secretly worked in a candy store during school recess and even began his newspaper round earlier to squeeze in some extra sales. He saved that extra money for future endeavours, while using a small amount to buy comic books and candy. He developed the discipline of hard work at this young age, a capability that would serve him in the future.

In pursuit of a better life, the Disney family moved to Chicago. Always eager to develop his craft, he drew cartoons for his new school newspaper. Unbeknownst to his family, he used his secret savings to pay for classes at the Chicago Academy of Fine Arts, building future capability as a cartoonist.

When he was sixteen, he was so eager to join the army that he forged papers and joined the Ambulance Corps. During his tour of duty in post-World War I France, he sketched wherever and on whatever he could. He used his ambulance as a blank canvas to sketch comical images to boost the spirits of the troops.

While many of his companions spent their spare time drinking and gambling, Walt focussed on his craft and developed an entrepreneurial flair. He often scoured abandoned battle fields for military junk, like German helmets, and sold them as war souvenirs. In doing so, he showcased another trait of permanent reinvention: using spare time to develop capabilities, without knowing how those capabilities might reward you in the future.

Pursuing a Vision

On his return to the United States, Walt dismissed the idea of a steady career to pursue his vision in the nascent animation industry. In 1920, his brother Roy helped him secure a job at the

Pesmen-Rubin Studio, where he further developed his capability as a cartoonist. Unfortunately, after only six weeks, the studio had to let him go due to a slowdown in bookings. During that brief period with Pesmen, he formed a crucial friendship with a gifted cartoonist named Ub Iwerks. Iwerks would prove to be a key character in the Disney success story.

The new friends formed Iwerks–Disney Commercial Artists, a venture they abandoned soon afterwards to pursue gainful employment with the Kansas City Slide Co. While working there, Disney offered to create a short cartoon for the Newman movie theatre. Even though the theatre refused, he created it anyway, knowing he would need to prove himself.

When they saw it, Newman agreed to pay for the production costs. Gaining in confidence, Disney went on to produce a successful series called the Newman Laugh-O-grams. Inspired by this modest success, at only twenty-two, he raised $15,000 (almost $250,000 in today's terms) to launch Laugh-O-gram Films. He hired a full team and secured a contract to produce an innovative new kind of short movie, 'Alice's Wonderland', in which a young girl filmed in live action interacted with animated characters.

The contract was only payable on delivery, which meant cash flow was minimal. Living on only a can of baked beans each day, he filmed live action by day and did the animation by night. He was riding on the crest of a wave until disaster struck when the company that commissioned the work went bankrupt. After two gruelling years of hard work, Laugh-O-gram Films joined them in bankruptcy.

Serendipity Strikes

Roy Disney had recently moved to Hollywood because the warm climate eased his tuberculosis. Walt wanted to join his brother to pursue his vision of becoming a Hollywood director, but couldn't afford a ticket. To earn the fare, he went door to door offering to make family movies. Eventually all he had left was his camera. He sold that too and bought a one-way ticket to Hollywood.

Before we continue, notice how he has been building his capability, skills and resilience. He was purposeful about making his success happen. He was driven by his passion and a vision that helped him endure the many obstacles that littered his path to success. Next, let's look at a series of broader movements plotted as S curve jumps.

When he joined his brother in Hollywood, a press pass from his Kansas days afforded him access to the Hollywood studios. Each day, he wandered the studios, looking for work and learning the inner workings of the studios, asking questions of directors, actors and distributors.

When no work materialised, he leaned on previous capability: his Alice showreel. His break eventually came when a New York distributor named Margaret Winkler commissioned twelve new Alice comedy shorts.

In 1924, with start-up capital from his uncle and support from his brother Roy, Disney Brothers Studio was born. Undeterred by his previous bankruptcy, he assembled an effective team, including his old friend Ub Iwerks and his future wife Lillian.

Disney had a great working relationship with Winkler, until she married Charles Mintz. Mintz took over the business relationship and contracted Disney Brothers Studio to create a twenty-six-part series of cartoons for Universal studios called 'Oswald the Lucky Rabbit'.

It was 1928, and Oswald proved more successful than anyone had imagined. Buoyed by the success of Oswald, Walt travelled to New York confident he could negotiate a better contract for all future Oswald productions. Mintz had other ideas. When Mintz offered a lesser contract, Walt threatened to take Oswald to another distributor. That's when Mintz reminded him that he owned all the rights to Oswald and Disney Brothers was just a contractor.

To make matters worse, Mintz had secretly persuaded some of the Disney animators to join his brand-new studio. With the promise of better conditions, many of them took the deal. Only

Figure 13.1 Di'S'ney curve 1

a few loyal members remained, including his wife Lillian and his best animator Ub. Such challenges are part of the pursuit of any vision, they are a rite of passage.

Notice how Walt's early-life experiences resulted in his first commercial S curve success. He learned a tough lesson: the necessity to jump to a new curve while you are enjoying the success of the existing one, not when encounter a crisis.

Walt vowed never again to produce cartoons for other studios. From that moment on, the Disney brothers would own their own productions. Armed with a new vision, the team developed a new cartoon. While Walt wanted to call it Mortimer Mouse, Lillian wisely convinced him to call it something else and so Mickey Mouse was born.

One hitch remained – they were still under a contractual obligation to deliver some remaining Oswald episodes to Mintz. They undertook to finish Oswald by day and secretly work on Mickey Mouse by night, thus working on a new curve while maintaining the current one.

The first two Mickey Mouse cartoons achieved only moderate success. The real breakthrough came in 1928 with the release

Figure 13.2   Di'S'ney curve 2

of 'Steamboat Willie', the first cartoon to include a synchronised soundtrack. With that Disney Brothers had their first hit.

Walt Disney was twenty-eight when Mickey Mouse became a cultural phenomenon. However, unlike Nokia and BlackBerry, Walt never stopped pushing the boundaries. Having learned from the Mintz experience, he enjoyed the success that Mickey Mouse delivered, but he continued to jump the curves and experiment.

The following part of the Disney evolution is crucial, but often glossed over, because it did not result in obvious commercial success. It did, however, deliver capabilities that would repay the studio handsomely in the future.

Silly Symphonies

Disney animators experimented with a release called 'The Skeleton Dance' as part of a lesser-known animated series called 'Silly Symphonies'. Silly Symphonies stretched the team's capabilities. In many ways, Silly Symphonies was like an innovation lab, where they could experiment with different themes and introduce new characters. The Silly Symphonies were a key step in the Disney curves. They gave the team capability that they would use in the future and, through these experiments, they developed a distinct identity. The experiments gave the team a new mindset and a laboratory to tinker with new technologies.

Mickey Mouse became the Disney cash cow. The studio soon optimised their production and the animation remained in black and white to keep costs low. The profits fuelled other experiments such as Silly Symphonies, the successful curve fuelled the future ones.

It is difficult for business leaders to reinvent ahead of the curve like Walt Disney and Fujifilm did. Often, they are under relentless pressure to deliver short-term results. Under such pressure, many business leaders would consider an experiment like the Silly Symphonies a financial failure. Many organisations would never have supported the project in the first place. Instead, they would focus on optimising the success of Mickey Mouse. The jump to a new curve would appear to be a step backwards, especially when it only results in capability.

Return on capability is intangible when we compare it to existing, established and proven business (and mental) models. This is why new business models require new measurements and new mindsets. When the business environment is in flux, we cannot measure future endeavours in the same way we measure past successes. When you embark on an experiment, you build capability and that capability can deliver unintended successes. This is like the apparent 'failure' of Amazon's Fire Phone, described in Chapter Two, which repaid the business with competitive advantage in voice technologies.

Notice how the S curve jumps in Figure 13.3 leap frog the Silly Symphonies. I do this to emphasise how we tend to

Figure 13.3   Di'S'ney curve 3

overlook such steps. Often, we label projects as failures based on traditional measures of success such as return on investment. In financial terms, the Silly Symphonies were costly and did not yield the same profit margin as Mickey Mouse, but they were a game-changer for Disney. The Silly Symphonies instilled fresh confidence, a new mindset and new skills in the Disney team.

Encouraged by these new capabilities, Disney studios experimented with colour, new animation techniques and a range of innovative processes, all of which would become hallmarks of a Walt Disney production. Such breakthroughs earned Walt twenty-two Oscars over his career. Most importantly, the Disney team built unique capability that would be used to break new technological boundaries. Uneasy with success, it was at this stage that Walt took a huge leap. Such stretches are brave and bold: when they pay off, they pay off big, but when they fail, they can sink organisations.

Figure 13.4   Di'S'ney curve 4

Disney's Folly

At the time, animations were used as warm-up entertainment for feature-length movies. Disney's decision to break that paradigm with the first ever full-length animated feature film was a bold bet. As with any paradigm shift, he had to overcome huge resistance to finance the vision. As we explored earlier, it can hurt deeply when the very people you expect to support you do not. In Walt's case when his brother and wife tried to talk him out of it, it was due to fear of failure. Put yourself in their shoes; you can empathise with them, after all, they had overcome so many challenges to get to the peak of the curve. I imagine them thinking, 'Could you please just sit still Walt, can't we just enjoy it for a while?' His family's resistance was the least of his challenges, as he discovered when the entire movie industry referred to his vision of a feature-length animated film as 'Disney's Folly'.

'Disney's Folly' was indeed a huge risk. If it flopped, Walt faced another bankruptcy, and this time he had a lot to lose. Like Henry Ford with his motorcar, Walt could not secure financial backing, so he had to mortgage his home. As is the case with most entrepreneurial ideas, they appear risky and uneconomic, and no one can see your vision as clearly as you can. However, as British philosopher Alfred North Whitehead has observed, 'Almost all new ideas have a certain aspect of foolishness when they are first produced'.

Snow White proved a tremendous success, with many reviewers hailing it as a genuine work of art. In financial terms, production costs consistently overran and totalled $1.5m, a massive sum for a feature film in 1937 and $27m in today's terms.

By now, he had developed a formula for success. Success involves continually investing in yourself and in your business ahead of the necessity and when you have the funds to do so. Yes, Snow White was a huge risk, but she delivered a massive return, grossing $8m ($140m in today's terms) in box office sales alone. By now, Walt Disney had grown accustomed to high-risk bets

Figure 13.5   Di'S'ney curve 5

and to delivering world firsts. Up until this point, the stakes were lower. He had built capability with the Silly Symphonies that paid the studio back with Snow White. Proving the point about building capability, you do it slowly over years when there is less pressure. In sport, you practice your skills on the training field, not under the stadium lights. In business, you build capability before you need it, so you remain ahead of the curve.

Snow White's success led to more feature-film productions, including *Pinocchio*, *Fantasia*, *Dumbo*, *Bambi*, *Alice in Wonderland* and *Peter Pan*. It also led to the studio's first live-action blockbuster, Treasure Island, another new S curve jump.

However, while Disney Studios enjoyed the peak of success atop the Snow White curve, Walt Disney was already preoccupied thinking about the next one. He used much of the profits from Snow White and the Seven Dwarfs to finance a new $4.5m studio in Burbank, California. Burbank would go on to deliver so much value to the organisation, but Walt kept striving for more.

Let's pause to imagine the validation Walt must have enjoyed when Snow White proved a success, and again when Burbank

Figure 13.6 Di'S'ney curve 6

delivered the goods. Even the best of us would kick back and enjoy the crest of the wave, but Walt was still driven by a burning childhood vision. That creative pursuit of an inner calling, that inkling deep within kept whispering to him – what about that theme park?

Despite the vindication of his 'Folly', when he proposed the concept of Disneyland, the Disney board rejected such diversification with staunch opposition. The leader of the resistance? None other than his brother Roy. In defiance, Walt mortgaged his life insurance, stock holdings, house and even household furniture. With that he purchased an orange grove and began the construction of a 185-acre amusement park. Another first of its kind.

When it opened in 1955, Disneyland was recognised as one of the world's most popular tourist attractions. Once again, he felt the discomfort of success, and Disney rolled the dice yet again and bought a second property in Florida in the 1960s.

Even when he died of lung cancer in 1966, at the age of sixty-five, he never stopped reinventing. He realised that once you stop evolving, you start dying. This is evident in this beautiful extract from a speech he delivered to the Society of Motion Picture Engineers in 1938, a speech aptly entitled 'Growing Pains':

'Our business has grown with and by technical achievements. Should this technical progress ever come to a full stop, prepare the funeral oration for our medium'.

Walt sums up the mindset of permanent reinvention perfectly – keep evolving.

Walt suffered many setbacks in his life, from bankruptcies to betrayals, world wars to union battles, his mother's untimely death and many more. When those closest to him did not support his vision, he maintained a relentless drive in the face of adversity.

While Walt Disney shows how a powerful vision can build an empire, our next case study is about individual permanent reinvention. When you read it, notice how our subject exemplifies the permanent reinvention mindset by setting a vision, overcoming setbacks, building capability before he needs it, and reinventing himself time and time again.

The stage is now set for Arnold Schwarzenegger.

Chapter Thirteen Takeaways

- Build capability before you need it: RoC – return on capability. This capability can often come from what others label as failures.
- Use your time wisely; yes enjoy life, but don't squander your time when you have it.
- Build new capability in parallel with your existing capability, experiment while you are successful.
- Never stop adding new skills, always stay hungry, and jump to a new curve when you have the luxury of time and other resources.
- Persevere. Others will doubt you and are incapable of seeing your vision; know that it is well intended, they often just want to protect you.
- Vision is crucial. It keeps you going when things do not appear to work out; the pursuit of a higher calling dampens disappointments.
- Never stop reinventing: it is an infinity curve, the highs will outweigh the lows.
- Not all experiments yield financial returns; sometimes the return is in capabilities, mindsets and skill sets.
- Diversify portfolios into analogous fields. When Walt Disney dreamed about theme parks, no one could see the link to animation.
- Walt Disney saw them all as entertainment. He could see the invisible line that connected the dots.

Considerations

For the individual

- Have you allowed yourself to become a victim of circumstance?

- Do you use your time wisely?
- Do you work hard on your vision?
- Do you develop capabilities before you need them?
- Would you concede to the rejection of others?
- Would you battle to achieve your vision?

For the organisation

- Do you have a 'Silly Symphony' project, an experimental canvas that does not have high financial expectations?
- How would you react if your experiment did not pay off?
- Can you spot analogous fields for your core products?
- What is your theme park, that adjacent area in which you could use your capabilities?

14

I'll be Back (Again and Again): 'S'chwarzenegger Curves

'For me life is continuously being hungry. The meaning of life is not simply to exist, to survive, but to move ahead, to go up, to achieve, to conquer'.
—Arnold Schwarzenegger

Arnold Schwarzenegger grew up in war-torn Austria, the son of Gustav, an alcoholic police chief and one-time member of the Nazi Party. Gustav wanted Arnold to follow in his footsteps and become a police officer and wished Arnold would be more like his soccer-playing brother. Arnold had other plans and wanted to leave Austria and pursue his mighty vision.

He conceived this vision when he was just fifteen. He was inspired by a bodybuilding magazine which featured a former champion bodybuilder, Reg Park, who went on to become a movie star. When Arnold saw this, he felt that inner calling, an inkling that change was afoot. He realised this might be his ticket to America. Reg Park had the plan all laid out and all Arnold had to do was follow that plan, easy right?

First, he would become the best bodybuilder in the world and then the highest-paid movie star of all time. Arnold's vison was so powerful that it gave him the mental strength to overcome years of resistance and ridicule by his father. Like Walt Disney before him, although his vision was clear he still had many obstacles to overcome.

When Gustav forced Arnold to join the army, it was another obstacle he had to surmount. How could Arnold have time to train to become Mr. Universe if he spent the entire day training with the army? Although it was intense physical training, it was the wrong kind of training and he struggled to find time because his workday began at five a.m. Driven by his dream, every evening as the soldiers hit the bed, Arnold hit the gym. He trained for hours in the evenings and got up before the others for some extra training in the mornings.

Once you commit to your vision, the universe conspires to present a plethora of opportunities. While he was still in the army, he was invited to compete in the junior Mr. Europe championship. This was in conflict with his army duties and if he went he could face severe penalties, including prison. He fought the

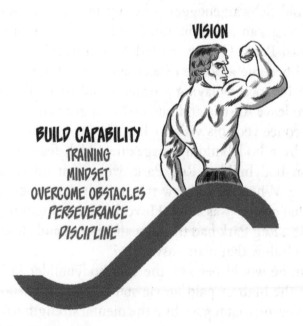

Figure 14.1   'S'chwarzenegger curve 1

mental dragons each night, but continually revisited his vision. In his mind's eye, he vividly rehearsed winning Mr. Universe; he visualised a telegram would arrive inviting him to America. When Arnold was crowned Mr. Universe, he was the youngest-ever winner at only twenty-one. The previous youngest winner was none other than Reg Park. He went on to win the title five times, and secured the Mr. Olympia title a record seven times.

'I always stay hungry, never satisfied with current accomplishments'.
—Arnold Schwarzenegger

Like Walt Disney before him, he had developed a winning formula. Vision, powered by hard work and perseverance, became the blueprint for his future achievements. Arnold credits that difficult time in the army as a foundational period. It was then that he built the capabilities of discipline, resilience and perseverance in the face of obstacles, skills that served him in every subsequent endeavour. This is an essential step in becoming undisruptable: enjoy your successes, but keep on learning, or as Arnold would say, 'Stay hungry'. For Arnold, becoming Mr. Universe was the top of his first curve. He used that winning formula to climb many curves thereafter and this is where his capability building gets interesting. This is the part of his success that is often glossed over, much like the Silly Symphonies step in Chapter Thirteen.

After securing the European Mr. Universe title for a second time, Arnold returned to his hotel room to find a telegram (the one he had envisioned every night). It was an invitation to compete in the American Mr. Universe competition, from Joe Weider, the creator of the contest, gym equipment, magazines and supplements. Weider was a key character in the Schwarzenegger story.

Arnold competed in Mr. Universe in Miami, but he didn't win. He was devastated; he felt his dream was falling apart. The next morning Weider invited him for breakfast and interviewed him for hours about his training techniques for his magazine.

Weider suggested that Arnold stay, he would give Arnold use of an apartment, a car and living expenses and in exchange Arnold could write articles promoting bodybuilding and sharing his training techniques.

After arriving in America, Arnold worked as a bricklayer to earn money because bodybuilding had not yet become a professional sport. Although he was the most recognisable figure in international bodybuilding, he had very little money. He chose bricklaying because it was a way to work out while earning money. He eventually built that side gig into a thriving business.

Writing articles by night, training and the physical toil of bricklaying was easy work in comparison to his time in the army. He didn't squander that extra energy, and invested even more time into his training. When he trained in the gym, people often asked why he trained with a smile on his face. He said that he smiled because he was incredibly grateful for this opportunity to pursue his vision and deep down he knew every repetition was one rep closer to achieving that vision. He needed to build capability for the next wave, while he rode the crest of the current one.

Arnold exemplified preparing for the next curve well ahead of the necessity to make the jump. When he had arrived in America, he'd studied how the U.S. economy worked so he could maximise the American Dream. Within two years, he had saved enough money to buy a six-unit apartment building, the start of the fortune he would accumulate from real estate investment. When he wrote articles for Weider, he built writing capability. With that capability, he produced a twenty-eight-page exercise booklet that he used to launch a highly successful mail-order fitness business and delivered paid seminars. His first book, *Arnold: The Education of a Bodybuilder*, was a best-seller when published in 1977 and, along with his *Encyclopaedia of Modern Bodybuilding* in 1985, has never been out of print since.

While he was exercising his entrepreneurial flair and training in the gym, Arnold built other capabilities he would need in the future. Most notably, he enrolled in acting classes, business

BUILD CAPABILITY
ACTING LESSONS
ENGLISH LESSONS
BUSINESS LESSONS
PROPERTY INVESTING
WRITING CAPABILITY

VISION

Figure 14.2   'S'chwarzenegger curve 2

classes and English lessons to build these skills in preparation for the next curve jump. The *LA Times* described Arnold's career as 'a series of stretching exercises, carefully calculated moves designed to first add bulk, as a box-office star, then definition, as a credible actor. With each movie, he says he tries to add a dimension'. What a perfect way to conceptualise capability-building. You first add bulk, then you add the definition: first you diverge to discover a skill you want to pursue, then you converge when you have found it.

When you share your vision with others, some people will discourage you to your face and others will mock you behind your back. Remember this is a rite of passage, if it was easy everyone would do it. Aristotle recognised this centuries ago when he said, 'To avoid criticism, say nothing, do nothing, be nothing'. Arnold's father ridiculed his vision to become a bodybuilder, now it was the turn of the general public to ridicule his dreams of becoming a movie star, but Arnold had developed great resilience to such discouragement.

Figure 14.3   'S'chwarzenegger curve 3

He explained how Hollywood reacted when he declared his ambitions to become a Hollywood movie star. 'That I was able to bridge over to acting even though the majority of people in Hollywood said it would never happen because of my accent, because of my body being overly developed, and because of my name – that people wouldn't be able to pronounce. All those kinds of excuses. So, I did not listen to the naysayers and was just going after my vision. I was very happy when it worked out'.

For those who are familiar with the Arnold Schwarzenegger story, you will know how he didn't stop evolving when he became one of the highest-paid movie stars of all time. His next curve was in politics, again using capability he had built while he enjoyed the peak of his acting curve.

In Chapter 13 we saw that, even after Walt Disney delivered the financial success of Snow White – dubbed Disney's Folly – he couldn't secure financial support for Disneyland. Even though he had succeeded with one vision, people still could not envisage his next one. Arnold was no different, but the support he lacked was moral support. Despite his successful transition from bodybuilding to acting, when he announced that he would run for office in California in 2003, many people ridiculed that vision too.

'When I wanted to be a public servant and serve the people of California, I also was able to do that even though everyone said it would never happen, and I didn't have the experience, and why would the people elect me? I didn't listen to the naysayers then either, and it happened'.

Despite all his successes, Arnold never allowed his victories to defeat him. He says, 'As soon as you think you are perfect, then you are screwed'. This is what happened to Jim Balsillie and BlackBerry. This is what happened to Nokia and Kodak. And this is what happens in the workplace, and will continue to happen more frequently today than at any other point in history. We must keep evolving.

In my rugby career, there were so many far more talented players than I ever was. Often the schoolboy heroes struggled greatly if they made it to the professional field. They had never learned the skill of discipline and hard work, never experienced the early setbacks that gift you with resilience. They presumed the talent that got them to the top would keep them there. These lessons translate into the professional environment too. As individuals we might stumble into a career in a growing industry and benefit from the growth of that field, but luck will not keep us competitive. As organisations, we may stumble upon a killer product, but defending that early advantage won't keep us ahead of the curve. This is ever more the case in a VUCA world in which we need a mix of hard work, vision and permanent reinvention to remain undisruptable.

Arnold Schwarzenegger exemplifies the permanent reinvention lens of vision and managing contrasts. Vision lives at the top of the S curve. However, so many individuals never get to attempt, let alone to achieve their vision because they are stricken by fear. Our final exemplar is an incredible story of finding opportunity in crisis, overcoming obstacles and facing fear.

Chapter Fourteen Takeaways

- The foundations for later success are developed through early life experiences.
- Vision drives you through the tough times.
- Visualisation is a powerful practice.
- Build capability before you need that capability.
- Use your time wisely, when you have it.
- Build new capability in parallel with your existing capability.
- Don't mind the naysayers, they cannot see what you see, there is nothing in a caterpillar that tells you it's going to be a butterfly.
- Never stop adding new skills, always stay hungry.

Considerations

For the individual

- Have you let yourself be a victim of your circumstances?
- Do you let the opinions of others discourage you? Roman emperor Marcus Aurelius spoke of 'The tranquillity that comes when you stop caring what they say. Or think or do. Only what You do'.

For the organisation

- Are your people developing new capabilities while maximising their current ones?
- Does your organisation explore future capabilities while exploiting current ones?

15

Cochrane Curves – Overcoming Crises and Fear

OPPORTUNITY IN CRISIS
OVERCOMING FEAR
NAVIGATING MALE DOMINATED SOCIETY
SURMOUNTING MANY OBSTACLES

Figure 15.1   Cochrane curves

'If I knew all I know today when I began to put the dish-washer on the market, I never would have had the courage to start. But then, I would have missed a very wonderful experience'.

—Josephine Cochrane

I grew up in a wonderfully wooded area in Ireland. We had two magnificent redwood (sequoia) trees in our garden. When I was about ten years old, I asked my father why the bark of a redwood is soft. He explained how the thick bark protects the tree from disease and provides a fire-resistant shell to shield the tree from forest fires. My childhood instinct was to think how this was terrible, we should protect the tree from the destructive fire; as it turned out, I was not alone in my reaction. Since the 1900s, man has tampered with natural fires to inhibit the resulting destruction. However, wildfires are essential for the renewal of natural ecosystems. If they don't occur, plants and trees may mature, deteriorate, or die without ever releasing their seed.

Trees, fauna and foliage in those forests prone to fires have evolved in fascinating ways. Some trees produce resin-coated cones containing mature seeds that are only activated when fire breaks out. The heat of the fire melts the resin around the cones, like the wax of a candle. This apparent act of destruction releases seeds that have been waiting patiently for their opportunity to germinate. Other forest plants contain seeds that have a thick outer coating – these seeds require fire to burn off their outer shell to release their kernel. This phenomenon provides a powerful metaphor how we must approach the crises we will inevitably encounter throughout periods of mass change.

When crises happen in life, they can feel devastating in the moment, but they can release latent potential. By shaking us from our existing paths, unforeseen paths are uncovered. Our parents and grandparents lived in the aftermath of the devastation of world wars while most of us have lived through a relatively stable period in human history. However, as the Covid-19 pandemic, socio-political turmoil, climate change and the 2008 financial downturn demonstrate, we are still susceptible to crises. According to IMD-Lausanne's Professor Jim Ellert[1], since 1988, the world has experienced 469 country recessions alone. Crises are a phenomenon that we have managed for millennia and we need to become comfortable with them once again. A permanent reinvention mindset is essential to reframe crises as opportunities. Crises reshuffle the tectonic plates of the economic landscape. To adapt and benefit from the change we must be flexible and ready. A crisis can be viewed as an opportunity or a danger, depending on one's perception about a situation. Sometimes the crisis reveals a path we would have never pursued without the push. This was certainly the case for the next undisruptable exemplar Josephine Garis Cochrane.

Josephine Garis was born in 1839. When she married William Cochran, she added an 'e' to Cochran to make her name more elegant. Indeed, the pursuit of an elegant lifestyle was high on the agenda for the Cochranes. William was a merchant, investor and rising politician, who made a modest fortune in the dry goods industry. William and Josephine led an uptown life of wealthy socialites in Shelby County, Illinois. They enjoyed throwing dinner parties to flaunt their lavish home, which boasted a set of heirloom China that reportedly dated back to the 1600s[2].

Josephine grew increasingly frustrated when servants chipped her prized China. Growing ever more frustrated, one day, she vowed that henceforth she alone would wash the China. After several washes she regretted her decision and resented the chore. It was in these moments that she daydreamed of an invention that would wash dishes without chipping them. Thus, her vision was born, but the road ahead would present many obstacles.

When she discussed her dishwashing invention with friends, they encouraged her to pursue the idea. She could use William's connections in a male-dominated society to fast-track her idea.

[1] http://iedc.si/blog/single-blog-post/iedc-wisdoms/2019/08/20/anticipating-the-next-global-financial-crisis-and-recession
[2] The Woman Who Invented The Dishwasher by Julie M. Fenster https://www.inventionandtech.com/content/woman-who-invented-dishwasher-1

However, fate had other plans. William had been suffering from ill health, partly due to his battle with alcoholism, and died suddenly. Josephine found herself widowed, but all was not lost, she could use William's estate to fund her new concept. However, William's affairs were far from orderly. In fact, he owed $2,769.77, or about $71,000 today. Her options were move in with relatives, find a job, or face staunch resistance as she pursued her vision. Luckily for Josephine, she had already started work on her invention, hammering away in the shed behind her house.

This apparent crisis was the catalyst required for Josephine's potential to emerge. She came from a long line of inventors and had innovation-rich blood coursing through her veins. Josephine's great-grandfather was John Fitch, the creator of America's first steamboats[3]. Meanwhile, both her parents exposed her to engineering from a young age. Her father had a portfolio of loosely connected capabilities; he worked in woollen mills, sawmills, gristmills and swamps. Growing up around this mindset rubbed off on Josephine because coming up with the invention proved to be the easy part. Gaining support, in a time when women were not easily accepted as innovators, was a huge obstacle to overcome. This was in nineteenth century America, when women still lacked the right to vote. Josephine had married right out of school at the age of nineteen. The odds of success were slim.

Josephine took her design to several male engineers who would not take it seriously because she lacked any mechanical training. She said, 'I couldn't get men to do the things I wanted in my way until they had tried and failed on their own. They knew I knew nothing, academically, about mechanics, and they insisted on having their own way with my invention until they convinced themselves my way was the better, no matter how I had arrived at it'. Eventually, she discovered and enlisted a young forward-thinking mechanic named George Butters, who would build the machine according to her design.

Josephine was not the first to invent a dishwashing machine. However, she was the first to use water pressure rather than

---

[3] https://www.uh.edu/engines/epi1397.htm

scrubbers to clean the dishes. She also designed racks to hold the dishes in place to avoid damage. In addition, previous washing machines required the user to pour boiling water over the dishes. In 1886, Josephine received U.S. patent no. 355,139 for her 'Dish Washing Machine'.

Receiving the patent proved only half the battle. Next Josephine had to find investors and customers. When she couldn't secure investment, she went to work selling her invention alone. She said of the challenge, 'When it comes to buying something for the kitchen that costs $75 or $100, a woman begins at once to figure out all the other things she could do with the money. She hates dishwashing – what woman does not? – but she has not learned to think of her time and comfort as worth money. Besides, she isn't the deciding factor when it comes to spending comparatively large sums of money for the house. Her husband sees that adversely, generally, in the case of costly kitchen conveniences – though he will put comptometers and all that into his office every day of the week without even mentioning the fact to her'. Unperturbed by the challenge, she targeted larger institutions, like restaurants and hotels. Finally, her big opportunity came when a friend introduced her to the manager of Chicago's Palmer House, one of the most famous hotels in the country. It is this part of her story that I want to emphasise – pursuing a vision not only involved overcoming obstacles, but many visions are stillborn by the fear of failure. So many great ideas never make it on to an S curve in the first place, but even when they do, the visionary still experiences fear. While Josephine had overcome countless setbacks thus far, she said this meeting was one of the hardest parts of her journey.

'You asked me what was the hardest part of getting into business', Mrs. Cochrane recalled for the reporter for the Record-Herald. 'That was almost the hardest thing I ever did, I think, crossing the great lobby alone. You cannot imagine what it was like in those days, twenty-five years ago, for a woman to cross a hotel lobby alone. I had never been anywhere without my husband or father – the lobby seemed a mile wide. I thought I should faint at every step, but I didn't – and I got an $800 order as my reward'.

Josephine never rested on her laurels – she went on to launch the Crescent Washing Machine Company, with none other than George Butters as manager. She died in 1913, at the ripe age of seventy-four, and received a further posthumous patent in 1917.

Fear naturally occurs when we have a vision for the future. Once we have the new idea, our 'change antibodies' activate and attack the new idea like the DNA of a caterpillar attacking an imaginal cell. When we anticipate and overcome this fear amazing things can unfold. Towards the end of her life, Josephine said of her adventure up the S curve: 'If I knew all I know today when I began to put the dishwasher on the market, I never would have had the courage to start. But then, I would have missed a very wonderful experience'.

There is one key lens of the permanent reinvention mindset that we have not yet visited. The companies and individuals who have successfully reinvented themselves have all exemplified this lens. In order to reinvent, you must let go of past achievements. In order to create something new, we need to let go of something old. This is the final lens for us to explore and a fitting way to close the book.

Chapter Fifteen Takeaways

- Crises can reveal emergent opportunities, sometimes it takes the crisis to unearth latent potential.
- With such a rapid rate of change we must become comfortable with crises.
- We are living in a period of unprecedented change, so we must be flexible and adaptable to change, which requires a change in mindset.
- Don't let fear kill your ideas – fear and change are bedfellows.
- Keep strong; fear will raise its head many times as you climb your curve.
- If Josephine Cochrane could overcome seemingly insurmountable obstacles, what excuse do we have?

Considerations

For the individual

- How have you reacted when you experienced a crisis in the past?
- Did the crisis reveal a path that you would not have otherwise considered?
- Think about the times you conquered fear, if you didn't do it, would you regret it today?

For the organisation

- When change presents obstacles, is your organisation taking the easy way out and accepting the excuses that fear offers?
- Are you dismissing great innovators because they do not have subject matter expertise, like Josephine did not have formal training as an engineer?

16

The Coconut Trap

Figure 16.1   The coconut trap

'Some of us think holding on makes us strong; but sometimes it is letting go'.

—Hermann Hesse

Many years ago, indigenous tribes used a clever technique to catch monkeys. They hollowed out a coconut and placed some fruit inside. Next, they would hang the coconut on a tree frequented by monkeys. In time, a monkey would come to investigate. The monkey would squeeze its hand into the coconut to grasp the bounty. In making a fist to grab the fruit, the monkey was trapped. His clenched fist no longer passed through the small opening. Even when faced with approaching captors, which could spell death or confinement, he maintained his grip. All he had to do was let go: letting go would mean freedom.

Like the monkey holding the fruit, many of us cling to the past with clenched fists. We clutch painful memories, we hold grudges, we harbour guilt. Equally, we defend successes, mental models and notions of grandeur. When we dwell on the past, we use up valuable energy which we could otherwise use to create our future.

In Chapter 6 we explored how vision pulls us forward as we climb the curve. However, when we pursue a vision of the future, it requires us to let go of certain aspects of the past; and therein lies a mammoth challenge.

Figure 16.2   Clinging to the past

'If you would make the most of yourself, cut away all of your vitality sappers; get rid of everything which hampers you and holds you back, everything which wastes your energy, cuts down your working capital. Get freedom at any cost'.

—Orison Swett Marden

A space shuttle uses considerably more energy to escape the gravitational drag of its home planet than it does travelling to its destination. This is why shuttle crews jettison fuel tanks once they reach a certain altitude. The shuttle requires a considerable amount of fuel to break free of its origin. When it approaches its destination, it benefits from a phenomenon known as gravity assistance, when the pilot uses the gravity of the destination planet to accelerate the spacecraft. Just like that destination planet, vision provides the gravity assistance we require to break free from the shackles of the past, but it takes considerably more effort to let go of the past than it does to embrace the future. Like the shuttle crew, we must jettison aspects of our past in order to enjoy our future.

You Are Not Your Jersey

'Avoid having your ego so close to your position that when your position falls, your ego goes with it'.

—Colin Powell

The New Zealand All Blacks (national rugby team) have a mantra: 'Leave the jersey in a better place'. It means, this is not your jersey, you are part of something bigger but do your best while you wear the jersey. It provides a valuable lesson about enjoying your moment in the sun but letting go to pursue another one once your time ends. When I played in Toulouse they had the same mindset. The club only contracted a certain number of players each year and there was a set number of locker spaces. Each locker was numbered in such a way that was not associated with an on-field jersey number and that was also the number you wore on your club sportswear. Some numbers were 00, others were 85 and mine was 71. When I joined, the coach explained to me in French that this was not my number, but I was part of a tradition that spanned decades. My interpretation still remains, 'You are not your jersey'.

Retirement can be a difficult time for all of us, particularly when we over-identify with our role. Just as with work retirement, many former athletes suffer from a loss of identity when they retire. Take, for example, how American football players retire on an average salary of two million dollars, yet eighty percent go broke soon afterwards. Some athletes cling to their old self and, in doing so, prevent the growth of a new self. 'Great men', the American sportswriter Mark Kram wrote, 'die twice – once as great, once as men'.

I count myself lucky because I suffered a raft of injuries and disappointments during my career which helped me realise that a sports career is just a cycle in a long life of cycles to come. This understanding is one of the most valuable gifts a career in sports has given me. It has inspired me to reinvent time and time again, with full confidence that there is no such thing as a failed attempt, unless you don't learn the lesson that the attempt imparts.

The coconut trap is not exclusive to the domain of professional sports. Everyone is susceptible: organisations, business professionals, and even parents. It is even more difficult for those people who achieve great success and recognition. The greater the success, the more difficult it can be to let go.

In a VUCA world, we require a portfolio of skills to survive disruption. This is why letting go of prior expertise and embracing constant learning is essential to the permanent reinvention mindset. As the Zen proverb goes, 'Knowledge is learning something new every day. Wisdom is letting go of something every day'. Becoming undisruptable isn't about being indispensable; it's about evolving throughout life. Once we feel the breeze of success, it's a signal to evolve and add some discomfort to the comfort. Everything has a decay rate: our achievements, our careers, our stations in life. As the prophetic science fiction writer Isaac Asimov observed, 'It is change, continuing change, inevitable change, that is the dominant factor in society today. No sensible decision can be made any longer without taking into account not only the world as it is, but the world as it will be'.

Systematic Abandonment

'There is nothing as difficult and as expensive, but also nothing as futile, as trying to keep a corpse from stinking'.
—Peter Drucker

Systematic abandonment is what author, Peter Drucker called the deliberate process of letting go of familiar products, services and business models in favour of exploring new or as yet unknown experiments. Painful as it was, Fujifilm embraced systematic abandonment while Kodak did not. Kodak is a posterchild of the coconut trap. They didn't fail because they were unaware of the future. They were magnificent innovators – they even invented the digital camera. Their fatal flaw was clinging too tightly to what they already knew. They were incapable of reallocating the adequate resources from the old world of analogue to the new world of digital. While Kodak squandered valuable time and energy clinging to past, like investment in analogue, Fujifilm systematically jettisoned whatever no longer served them and aggressively reallocated resources to the future.

Arnold Schwarzenegger let go of each of his previous achievements to make room for the future. He also let go of tragic mistakes, such as his extramarital affair, although it was a struggle, 'I can beat myself up as much as I want – it's not gonna change the situation. So the key thing is, how do you move forward?'

Walt Disney struggled to let go of the guilt over the death of his mother due to carbon monoxide poisoning in her new home. He blamed himself because he paid for the new house in which she died. Professionally, he was a master of letting go, as he evolved through his career from being an animator all the way through to becoming the evangelist. One story tells of how a child stopped him in Disneyland and asked, 'Hey mister, are you the Walt Disney?'. Walt's answer said a lot about letting go, with a smile he replied that he was no longer Walt Disney, today Walt Disney was a company; Walt Disney had become a brand.

As for Jospehine Cochrane, she let go of a future she did not want. When faced with the crisis of her husband's death and the residual debt, she made a decision. She decided she didn't want to maintain the persona that she once was, but instead she would create a new one.

As professionals, our careers end. As parents, our kids leave the nest. As organisations, our business models expire. When we continually evolve our vision of the future, it makes letting go of the past easier. Instead of being snagged like a monkey in a coconut trap, we can swing freely from curve to curve like a monkey swinging across the vines of life. We need to break off the wing-mirrors and live life by looking forward.

The Flight of the Butterfly

'There are far better things ahead than any we leave behind'.
—C. S. Lewis

When I retired from sport, I didn't have any problem letting go of who I used to be, but I did have problems letting go of some aspects of that past. I clung to feelings of underachievement. I often wondered what if I had not been injured? What if I joined this club instead of that one? What if I did this or that? I wasted a lot of mental energy dwelling on past decisions. Eventually, I realised how my rugby career had provided so many capabilities that would fuel a new future for myself. Even the painful experiences played their part. When I let go of certain elements of the past, I freed up cognitive capacity to create the future. Many opportunities came from that new capacity, perhaps even this book.

Once I learned about the metamorphosis of the butterfly, I discovered a perfect analogy for permanent reinvention for organisations, individuals and life. The death of the former self does not mean that the old us was not useful. Our former selves helped us get to where we are today. As an organisation, the legacy organisation provides resources to generate an emergent organisation. As professionals, all the skills we learn accumulate to give us a unique combination. In life, every lens we collect provides us with a unique worldview. We started our journey with the birth of the caterpillar, let's end it now with the flight of the butterfly.

The final stage of the metamorphosis of the caterpillar into a butterfly is the most beautiful. When the butterfly emerges from the cocoon, it holds on tightly for a moment, as it gazes longingly into the cocoon. The cells of the caterpillar have nourished the butterfly to fuel this new and evolved being. It is as if the butterfly holds the cocoon in a moment of gratitude, thanking its former self

Figure 16.3 'Flight of the Butterfly'

for the contribution toward its new becoming. After this moment of thanks, the butterfly lets go of the past and flies into the future.

This leaves us with only one question.

Would you rather be defined by a record of your past or driven by a vision of your future?

Chapter Sixteen Takeaways

- A space shuttle uses more fuel leaving its origin than it does arriving at its destination; we do the same when we cling to past achievements and painful memories.
- When we let go, we free up cognitive energy that we can use to create the future.
- Exemplars of permanent reinvention all let go of the past, Arnold and Walt let go of painful memories, but they also let go of past successes: they built upon them, rather than resting their laurels upon them.
- Fujifilm let go of their previous identity and reallocated resources to the future.
- The past fuels our present in all aspects of life: the legacy organisation fuels the emergent one, the old self fuels the new.
- A caterpillar starts life by eating its shell, using it as fuel, the butterfly uses the caterpillar as fuel and, in a final moment before taking flight, the butterfly holds on to the cocoon in a moment of gratitude before taking flight into the future.
- Do you want to be defined by your record of the past or driven by your vision for the future?

Reflections

For the individual

- What are you holding on to?
- Does it steal your energy?

- What would happen if you reallocated that energy to create something new?
- Are you holding on to some expertise or status, in the full knowledge that your role is in decline? If yes, what are you doing about it?
- How have you allowed yourself to be defined by your record of the past?
- How will you be driven by your vision of the future?

For the organisations

- Are you 'trying to keep a corpse from stinking'?
- How can you embrace systematic abandonment?
- When you encounter resistance, have you examined the full spectrum of reasons? Are executives resisting for their own personal reasons or do they have a valid reason to hold on to an existing product, service or business model?
- What about modes of thinking, are you holding on to analogue thinking in a digital world?
- How are you allowing your organisation to be defined by past achievements?
- How can you enable your organisation to be driven by a vision of the future?

References

Chapter 1: Resistance to Reinvention

90% of people won't change, Edward Miller, former CEO of Johns
Hopkins Medicine: Change or Die (Regan, 2007) https://www.amazon.
co.uk/Change-Die-Three-Keys-Work/dp/0061373672/
Causes of death: https://ourworldindata.org/causes-of-death
https://www.weforum.org/agenda/2020/05/how-many-people-die-
each-day-covid-19-coronavirus/
https://en.wikipedia.org/wiki/Peter_Medawar

Chapter 2: Kintsugi Thinking

Jeff Bezos 2015 letter to shareholders https://www.sec.gov/Archives/
edgar/data/1018724/000119312516530910/d168744dex991.htm
Diana Kander: Professional AF S3 | E8: The Amazon Fire Phone with
Ian Freed https://dianakander.com/podcast/

Chapter 3: S Curves: A Framework for Permanent Reinvention

Diffusion of Innovations, 5th Edition – Everett M. Rogers, 17 Nov. 2003
Disrupt Yourself, With a New Introduction: Master Relentless Change
and Speed Up Your Learning Curve - Whitney Johnson, Harvard
Business Review Press; Illustrated edition (2019)
The Innovator's Dilemma: When New Technologies Cause Great Firms
to Fail – Clayton M. Christensen, Harvard Business Review Press
https://venturebeat.com/2019/09/25/the-alexa-skills-store-now-has-
more-than-100000-voice-apps/

Jamie Dimon quote: https://reports.jpmorganchase.com/investor-relations/2019/ar-ceo-letters.htm

John F. Kennedy's State of the Union address, January 11, 1962: https://youtu.be/QDuEjZ3tSQM?t=224

Stall Points: Most Companies Stop Growing Yours Doesn't Have To – Matthew S. Olson and Derek van Bever, Yale University Press (April 28, 2008)

https://voicebot.ai/2021/01/14/alexa-skill-counts-surpass-80k-in-us-spain-adds-the-most-skills-new-skill-introduction-rate-continues-to-fall-across-countries/

Chapter 4: The Ouroboros: Infinity Curve

One from Many: VISA and the Rise of Chaordic Organization – Dee Hock https://www.amazon.co.uk/dp/B00XAX5VI0/r

Chapter 5: Recalibrating Time

Oldest Trees: https://www.livescience.com/29152-oldest-tree-in-world.html#:~:text=But%20which%20tree%20has%20been,the%20age%20of%20another%20P

Dr Robert Ballard: http://54.198.197.222/autodoc/page/bal0int-5

Spell of the Sensuous: Perceptions – David Abram, p. 133, Random House (2020)

Chapter 6: The Wasp Trap: Personal Vision

Chitin: https://www.sciencedirect.com/topics/agricultural-and-biological-sciences/chitin

Wasp Life Cyle: https://www.nbcenvironment.co.uk/residential/wasp-lifecycle/#:~:text=Each%20wasp%20goes%20through%20complete,be%20her%20first%20worker%20wasps

Wasp Pheromones: https://www.researchgate.net/publication/308959104_Conservation_of_Queen_Pheromones_Across_Two_Species_of_Vespine_Wasps

Retirement Study: https://www.nber.org/papers/w24127.pdf

Basketball Study: https://www.nytimes.com/2014/02/23/sports/olympics/olympians-use-imagery-as-mental-training.html

Jack Nicklaus, Golf My Way, Simon & Schuster; Revised edition (November 1, 2007)

Apple Valuation: https://www.nytimes.com/2020/08/19/technology/apple-2-trillion.html

Chapter 7: All Roads Lead to Rome: Organisational Vision

Archimedes: http://web.mit.edu/2.009/www/experiments/deathray/10_ArchimedesResult.html

Apple Stock: https://www.macrotrends.net/stocks/charts/AAPL/apple/stock-price-history

Steve Jobs Unveiling the Digital Hub Strategy, Jan 2001: https://www.youtube.com/watch?v=lmvmtmqqbeI

Chapter 8: Managing Contrasts

Rick Hansen: http://www.rickhanson.net/books/hardwiring-happiness/

80% of New Year's resolutions fail: https://health.usnews.com/health-news/blogs/eat-run/articles/2015-12-29/why-80-percent-of-new-years-resolutions-fail

Chapter 9: Crab Curves

Cells: https://theconversation.com/mapping-the-100-trillion-cells-that-make-up-your-body-103078

https://journals.plos.org/plosbiology/article?id=10.1371/journal.pbio.1002533

https://www.cell.com/cell/fulltext/S0092-8674(05)00408-3

Jack Welch quote on people moving on, 'Total Rethink: Why Entrepreneurs Should Act Like Revolutionaries' – David McCourt, Wiley (2019)

Happy Customers: https://phys.org/news/2019-10-happy-workers-productive.html

Jeff Bezos interview: https://www.youtube.com/watch?v=KPbKeNgh RYE

McKinsey, The do-or-die struggle for growth, August 1, 2005 https://www.mckinsey.com/featured-insights/employment-and-growth/the-do-or-die-struggle-for-growth#

https://www-bbc-co-uk.cdn.ampproject.org/c/s/www.bbc.co.uk/news/amp/business-55912878

Chapter 10: Here Be Dragons

Here Be Dragons: https://www.theatlantic.com/technology/archive/2013/12/no-old-maps-actually-say-here-be-dragons/282267/

Waters, Hannah (October 15, 2013). 'The Enchanting Sea Monsters on Medieval Maps'. Smithsonian Institution

Joseph Campbell, Dragon: https://www.youtube.com/watch?v=8IgGtGZwlDY

David Bowie Interview: https://www.youtube.com/watch?v=cNbnef_eXBM

'Assessment and prediction of stress-related growth'. Journal of Personality. PTG http://citeseerx.ist.psu.edu/viewdoc/download?doi=10.1.1.464.7125&rep=rep1&type=pdf

Chapter 11: The Immortal Jellyfish: Fujifilm

Fujifilm Covid-19 vaccine: https://www.fujifilm.eu/ie/covid-19

Innovating Out of Crisis: How Fujifilm Survived (and Thrived) As Its Core Business Was Vanishing – Shigetaka Komori, Stone Bridge Press (2015)

Lego Math Problem: http://web.math.ku.dk/~eilers/lego.html

Silver Crisis 1970s: https://priceonomics.com/how-the-hunt-brothers-cornered-the-silver-market/

https://www.fujifilm.com/sg/en/consumer/skincare/astalift

https://www.straitstimes.com/business/companies-markets/ceos-facelift-for-fujifilm-includes-cosmetics-business

https://www.fujifilmhealthcare.com/fujifilms-facts-and-figures

'How to anticipate wrenching change: CEOs can avoid being blindsided if they heed key signals'. – Leonard Fuld The Free Library, 2004 Chief Executive Publishing https://www.thefreelibrary.com/How+to+anticipate+wrenching+change%3a+CEOs+can+avoid+being+blindsided...-a0122411296

Andy Jassy Interview: https://techcrunch.com/2016/07/02/andy-jassys-brief-history-of-the-genesis-of-aws/

Amazon Earnings call Q2 2020, https://s2.q4cdn.com/299287126/files/doc_financials/2020/Q1/Amazon-Q1-2020-Earnings-Release.pdf

Staircases to growth, By Charles Conn, Robert J. McLean, Mehrdad Baghai, Stephen C. Coley and David White (November 1, 1996) McKinsey, https://www.mckinsey.com/featured-insights/employment-and-growth/staircases-to-growth

Chapter 12: Defeated by Victory: Nokia

Nokia's history: https://web.archive.org/web/20090223193956/http://www.nokia.com/about-nokia/company/story-of-nokia/nokias-first-century/the-merger

Nokia CEO throws iPhone: https://youtu.be/owvtKGlYFVA

https://arstechnica.com/gadgets/2008/06/us-smartphone-market-share-down-for-apple-in-2008/ https://www.nytimes.com/2010/09/27/technology/27nokia.html

Rita McGrath on Nokia on the Innovation Show: https://soundcloud.com/theinnovationshow/ep-237-end-of-competitive

https://theinnovationshow.io/episode/ep-237-end-of-competitive-advantage-how-to-keep-your-strategy-moving-as-fast-as-your-business-with-rita-mcgrath/

https://macdailynews.com/2007/02/12/rim_co_ceo_doesnt_see_threat_from_apples_iphone/

Jim Balsillie: https://www.youtube.com/watch?v=wQRcEObmSRM&t=1s

https://www.blackberry.com/content/dam/blackberry-com/Documents/pdf/financial-reports/2020/q4y2020/BlackBerry-Annual-Report%20 10-K%20.pdf

https://www.nokia.com/system/files/2020-02/nokia_results_2019_q4.pdf

Chapter 13: Di'S'ney Curves

Entrepreneurship, The Disney Way – Michael G. Goldsby

https://www.latimes.com/archives/la-xpm-1989-09-03-ca-2347-story.html

Walt Disney history: https://www.waltdisney.org

Inflation calculator: https://www.in2013dollars.com/us/inflation/1922?amount=15000

How Walt Disney funded his dream, https://www.huffpost.com/entry/how-walt-disney-funded-his-dream_b_5a38ebc1e4b0578d1 beb72a1

Chapter 14: I'll Be Back (Again and Again): 'S'chwarzenegger Curves

LA Times article: https://www.latimes.com/archives/la-xpm-1989-09-03-ca-2347-story.html

Total Recall: My Unbelievably True Life Story Paperback – Arnold Schwarzenegger, Simon & Schuster (November 5, 2013)

Arnold Schwarzenegger quotes on discouragement:

https://www.businessinsider.com/arnold-schwarzenegger-hollywood-told-him-he-would-never-act-2015-6

Chapter 15: Cochrane Curves – Overcoming Crises and Fear

Anticipating the Next Global Financial Crisis and Recession - Jim Ellert: http://iedc.si/blog/single-blog-post/iedc-wisdoms/2019/08/20/ anticipating-the-next-global-financial-crisis-and-recession

The Woman Who Invented The Dishwasher by Julie M. Fenster: https://www.inventionandtech.com/content/woman-who-invented-dishwasher-1

Inflation calculator $2,770 today. https://www.in2013dollars.com/us/ inflation/1880?amount=2770

https://www.uh.edu/engines/epi1397.htm

Chapter 16: The Coconut Trap

Hunting Monkeys: https://www.youtube.com/watch?v=9jBgo7UipqY

NFL Study, https://www.forbes.com/sites/leighsteinberg/2015/02/09/ 5-reasons-why-80-of-retired-nfl-players-go-broke/#227b7d4078cc

Arnold Schwarzenegger Regrets: https://www.vanityfair.com/news/ 1990/06/arnold-schwarzenegger-199006

Fujifilm, https://www.i-cio.com/strategy/digitalization/item/fujifilm-maxim-never-stop-transforming

Entrepreneurship the Disney Way 1st Edition - Michael Goldsby, Routledge; 1st edition (November 13, 2018)

Acknowledgments

This book is the collective wisdom of every fantastic guest who I've had the pleasure to host on the innovation show. It's the collective experience of clients I've worked with from Pfizer to Mastercard to Epic Games. It's the scar tissue of experiences from making leaps from one curve to the next and the lessons I've learned from every disappointment, every setback and every success. I thank those people who encouraged me on the various curves and those who did not; they also played an important role.

Special thanks to the brilliant people who provided feedback as I wrote this book. Ed Hess, if feedback is the food of champions, I have feasted like a champion. Charles Conn, your understanding of strategy, nature and humanity was an immense help. Anne Janzer, thank you for your guidance, expertise and encouragement. Whitney Johnson, your crucial feedback made this a better book, thank you. To my accountability partners, Carlo Pignataro, Morgan Cummins, Phillip Matthews and Andrew Macadam, my sincere thanks to you all. To the fantastic Fintan Taite, your illustrations are wonderful, thanks for your brilliant work. To my mentor Mick Kearney, thank you for everything my friend.

A special thanks to Dee Hock, who not only wrote the phenomenal Foreword for this book, but at 93, still serves as an inspiration to me and so many others. Dee, you were so far ahead of your time.

Thank you to those people who influenced my writing: Dee Hock, Charles Handy, Whitney Johnson, Mark Johnson, Scott D. Anthony, Michele Wucker, Greg Satell, Francesca Gino, Mark

Johnson, Robert Sapolsky, Rita McGrath, Michael Roberto, Maya Angelou, E.O. Wilson, James Baldwin and so many more.

To the Wiley team, Annie Knight, Katy Smith, Kelly Labrum and Deborah Schindler, thanks for taking a punt on me.

About the Author

Aidan McCullen reinvented himself after a ten-year rugby career with over one hundred caps for Leinster, Toulouse and London Irish and is a full Ireland Rugby International.

He worked in digital and innovation transformation and now works on culture and leadership initiatives after he discovered that you cannot change business models until you first change mental models.

He is the host and founder of the Global Innovation Show, which boasts Bill Gates as a listener and advocate. The show is broadcast on national radio in Ireland and the only English-speaking show on Finland's Business FM The show is available everywhere you find podcasts.

He developed and delivers a module on Emerging Technology Trends in Trinity College Business School, ranked first in Ireland and in the top one hundred globally.

Aidan speaks globally on disruption and change for organisations such as Mastercard, Google, Epic Games and many more. He runs workshops on permanent reinvention, bias and communication.

He is also a board director for National Broadband Ireland. Please visit www.aidanmccullen.com for more information.

Index